I0018978

Identity Threat Detection and Response

James Relington

Copyright © 2025 James Relington

All rights reserved

DEDICATION

This book is dedicated to all the professionals working tirelessly to secure digital identities and protect organizations from ever-evolving threats. To the cybersecurity teams, IT administrators, and identity management experts who ensure safe and seamless access for users—your work is invaluable. And to my family and friends, whose support and encouragement made this journey possible, thank you.

AKNOWLEDGEMENTS

I would like to express my deepest gratitude to everyone who contributed to the creation of this book. To my colleagues and mentors in the cybersecurity and identity management field, your insights and expertise have been invaluable. To the organizations and professionals who shared their experiences and best practices, your contributions have enriched this work. A special thanks to my family and friends for their unwavering support and encouragement throughout this journey. Finally, to the readers, thank you for your interest in identity lifecycle management—may this book help you navigate the evolving landscape of digital security with confidence.

Introduction to Identity Threat Detection and Response

Identity threats have become one of the most pressing security concerns for organizations across all industries. As cybercriminals continue to refine their attack techniques, identity-based threats have emerged as a primary vector for gaining unauthorized access to sensitive systems and data. Traditional security models that focus solely on perimeter defenses are no longer sufficient, as attackers often exploit compromised credentials to bypass security controls. This has led to a paradigm shift in cybersecurity, where identity threat detection and response (ITDR) is now a critical component of an organization's overall security strategy.

At its core, identity threat detection and response involves monitoring, analyzing, and mitigating risks associated with identity-related threats. This includes unauthorized access attempts, credential theft, account takeovers, privilege escalation, and insider threats. Unlike traditional security approaches that focus on detecting malware or network intrusions, ITDR is centered on understanding user behaviors, analyzing access patterns, and identifying anomalies that may indicate malicious activity. By taking an identity-centric approach to security, organizations can detect threats earlier in the attack chain and respond more effectively to mitigate potential damage.

The rise of identity-related attacks can be attributed to several factors. First, the widespread adoption of cloud services, remote work, and digital transformation initiatives has significantly expanded the attack surface. Employees, contractors, and third-party vendors access corporate systems from various locations and devices, making it more challenging to enforce security policies consistently. Second, attackers have recognized that stealing or compromising legitimate credentials is often easier than breaching network defenses. Techniques such as phishing, credential stuffing, and social engineering allow adversaries to obtain valid credentials and operate within an organization's environment without immediately triggering alarms.

One of the key challenges in detecting identity threats is distinguishing between legitimate user activity and malicious behavior. Users often access multiple applications and systems throughout their workday, and their behavior can vary based on context, role, and location. To address this challenge, organizations are increasingly leveraging user behavior analytics (UBA) and machine learning to detect anomalies. These technologies analyze vast amounts of data to establish a baseline of normal user activity and flag deviations that could indicate a security incident. For example, if an employee suddenly logs in from an unfamiliar location, attempts to access sensitive files they have never interacted with before, or performs actions outside their typical work hours, these behaviors may warrant further investigation.

Another critical aspect of identity threat detection and response is privileged access management (PAM). Privileged accounts, such as those belonging to system administrators, database managers, or security teams, are high-value targets for attackers. Once compromised, these accounts can be used to move laterally across an organization's network, escalate privileges, and exfiltrate data without detection. Implementing robust PAM solutions helps restrict access to sensitive systems, enforce least privilege principles, and monitor privileged session activities to detect and respond to suspicious actions in real time.

Identity threats are not limited to external adversaries; insider threats pose a significant risk as well. Whether intentional or accidental, employees, contractors, or business partners can misuse their access privileges to compromise security. In some cases, insiders may steal data for personal gain, while in others, they may unintentionally expose credentials or sensitive information due to negligence. Effective ITDR strategies must account for insider threats by continuously monitoring access behavior, setting up alerts for unusual activity, and enforcing strict access controls to minimize the risk of abuse.

The increasing reliance on identity federation and single sign-on (SSO) solutions has also introduced new security challenges. While these technologies enhance user convenience and streamline authentication processes, they can become a single point of failure if not properly secured. A compromised SSO account can grant an attacker access to multiple applications, making it essential to implement strong authentication mechanisms, such as multi-factor authentication (MFA), to reduce the risk of identity compromise. Additionally, organizations must continuously monitor federated identities for signs of unauthorized access or abuse.

Incident response is a critical component of ITDR, as early detection alone is not enough to prevent damage. Organizations must establish well-defined incident response procedures to quickly contain and mitigate identity-related security incidents. This involves automating response actions, such as temporarily disabling compromised accounts, forcing password resets, or revoking access to critical systems when a potential threat is detected. Security teams must also conduct forensic investigations to determine the root cause of identity breaches, assess the extent of the compromise, and implement corrective measures to prevent future incidents.

The integration of ITDR with other security frameworks, such as Security Information and Event Management (SIEM) and Extended Detection and Response (XDR), enhances an organization's ability to detect and respond to identity threats holistically. By correlating identity-related events with network, endpoint, and cloud security data, security teams can gain deeper visibility into attack patterns and take proactive measures to prevent breaches. The use of automation and artificial intelligence further strengthens ITDR by reducing the time it takes to detect and respond to identity threats, allowing security teams to focus on high-priority incidents.

As identity threats continue to evolve, organizations must adopt a proactive approach to identity security. This requires continuous monitoring, risk-based access controls, and adaptive authentication mechanisms to ensure that users and systems are protected against identity-related attacks. By implementing a comprehensive ITDR strategy, organizations can not only detect and respond to identity threats more effectively but also enhance their overall cybersecurity posture.

The Evolution of Identity-Based Attacks

Identity-based attacks have evolved significantly over the past few decades, transforming from simple password guessing attempts to sophisticated, multi-stage operations that leverage automation, artificial intelligence, and social engineering. As digital transformation accelerates and organizations continue to move to the cloud, the attack surface for identity threats has expanded dramatically. Cybercriminals now have more opportunities than ever to exploit weaknesses in identity and access management systems, making identity security one of the most critical aspects of modern cybersecurity defense strategies.

Early identity-based attacks were largely opportunistic and relied on rudimentary techniques. In the early days of computing, attackers would attempt to gain access to systems using default passwords or weak, easily guessable credentials. This method, known as brute-force attacks, involved systematically trying different password combinations until the correct one was found. While effective in some cases, brute-force attacks were time-consuming and required significant computing power as password complexity increased.

As organizations became more aware of password security, attackers shifted their focus to credential theft. One of the earliest and most common methods of stealing credentials was keylogging, where malware was used to record keystrokes and capture user login information. Keyloggers were often distributed through malicious email attachments, infected software downloads, or compromised websites. Once installed on a victim's device, the malware would silently record login credentials and send them to an attacker, enabling unauthorized access to sensitive accounts and systems.

The rise of phishing marked a significant turning point in identity-based attacks. Instead of relying on technical exploits, phishing attacks targeted human psychology, tricking users into voluntarily providing their login credentials. Attackers would create fake login pages that closely resembled legitimate websites and lure victims into entering their usernames and passwords. These attacks were often delivered through deceptive emails that appeared to come from trusted sources, such as banks, social media platforms, or corporate IT departments. As phishing techniques became more sophisticated, attackers started using spear-phishing, which involved highly targeted and personalized attacks designed to deceive specific individuals within an organization.

With the widespread adoption of cloud computing and online services, credential stuffing became another major threat. Credential stuffing attacks take advantage of the fact that many users reuse passwords across multiple accounts. When a data breach exposes a set of usernames and passwords, attackers use automated scripts to test those credentials across different platforms, hoping that victims have used the same login information elsewhere. The effectiveness of credential stuffing has been amplified by the vast amount of stolen credentials available on the dark web, often obtained from large-scale data breaches affecting major companies.

Another major evolution in identity-based attacks is the rise of account takeovers (ATO). In an ATO attack, cybercriminals gain unauthorized access to a user's account and use it for malicious purposes. This could include making fraudulent transactions, exfiltrating sensitive data, or using the account to launch further attacks. ATOs have become particularly dangerous in the financial and e-commerce sectors, where stolen accounts can be monetized easily. Attackers use a variety of techniques to conduct ATOs, including social engineering, phishing, and exploiting weak authentication mechanisms.

The introduction of multi-factor authentication (MFA) was intended to counteract these attacks by adding an extra layer of security beyond passwords. However, attackers quickly adapted by developing new methods to bypass MFA. One such method is SIM swapping, where attackers trick or bribe mobile carriers into transferring a victim's phone number to a new SIM card under their control. With access to the victim's phone number, attackers can intercept SMS-based authentication codes and gain control over their accounts. Another method involves using real-time phishing kits that capture MFA tokens in addition to usernames and passwords, allowing attackers to bypass authentication in real time.

The emergence of business email compromise (BEC) attacks represents another evolution in identity-based threats. BEC attacks do not rely on malware or brute-force techniques but instead exploit human trust. In a BEC attack, an attacker impersonates a high-ranking executive or business partner and tricks employees into transferring money or revealing sensitive information. These attacks often use advanced social engineering tactics, such as spoofed email domains and carefully crafted messages, to manipulate victims into taking actions that benefit the attacker.

As artificial intelligence and machine learning become more prevalent, attackers are leveraging these technologies to enhance identity-based attacks. AI-driven attacks can automate phishing campaigns, generate highly convincing deepfake voice or video impersonations, and analyze stolen credentials to optimize credential stuffing operations. The use of AI also allows attackers to conduct more effective social engineering attacks by analyzing publicly available data and crafting highly personalized messages that increase the likelihood of success.

The shift toward identity federation and single sign-on (SSO) has introduced new challenges in identity security. While these technologies improve user convenience by reducing the number of passwords needed, they also create a single point of failure. If an attacker compromises an identity provider's credentials, they can gain access to multiple applications and services. Attackers have recognized this vulnerability and increasingly target SSO platforms, making it crucial for organizations to implement strong authentication measures and continuously monitor access logs for suspicious activity.

Insider threats have also evolved alongside external identity-based attacks. While traditional insider threats involved disgruntled employees stealing company data, modern insider threats are more complex. Some insiders are recruited by cybercriminal organizations or nation-state actors to provide access to sensitive systems in exchange for financial compensation. Others unintentionally compromise security by falling victim to phishing scams or failing to follow security best practices. Organizations must adopt a proactive approach to insider threat detection by monitoring user behavior and identifying deviations from normal activity patterns.

The increasing reliance on cloud services, remote work, and third-party integrations has further expanded the identity attack surface. Attackers no longer need to breach on-premises networks to access critical systems; they can exploit weak cloud security configurations, steal API keys, or compromise third-party service providers. This shift has forced organizations to rethink their security strategies and adopt a Zero Trust approach, which assumes that no user or device should be inherently trusted, regardless of their location or network environment.

As identity-based attacks continue to evolve, organizations must stay ahead of emerging threats by continuously adapting their security strategies. Implementing strong authentication mechanisms, leveraging AI-driven threat detection, and adopting a Zero Trust security model are essential steps in mitigating identity threats. Cybercriminals will continue to refine their techniques, making it imperative for security teams to remain vigilant, educate users, and invest in advanced identity threat detection and response capabilities.

Understanding the Modern Threat Landscape

The modern cybersecurity threat landscape is more complex and dynamic than ever before. As organizations embrace digital transformation, cloud computing, remote work, and interconnected systems, the attack surface continues to expand. Cybercriminals, state-sponsored actors, and insider threats leverage sophisticated techniques to exploit vulnerabilities in identity and access management, network security, and software applications. Traditional security models, which relied heavily on perimeter defenses, are no longer sufficient in protecting against modern threats. Attackers now use identity-based methods to infiltrate systems, bypass security controls, and persist within organizations for extended periods without detection. Understanding the evolving nature of these threats is critical for organizations seeking to protect their data, users, and infrastructure.

One of the most significant shifts in the threat landscape is the increased reliance on stolen or compromised credentials. Attackers no longer need to break into networks through brute-force methods or malware when they can simply log in using valid but stolen credentials. Cybercriminals have developed extensive underground marketplaces where compromised credentials are bought and sold in bulk. These credentials often come from large-scale data breaches affecting social media platforms, cloud storage services, and corporate databases. Once attackers gain access to a valid account, they can escalate privileges, move laterally within the environment, and exfiltrate sensitive information without triggering alarms.

The rise of ransomware has further intensified security concerns across industries. In the past, ransomware primarily targeted individual users by encrypting their files and demanding a ransom for decryption. Today, ransomware operators conduct highly targeted attacks against enterprises, healthcare providers, government agencies, and critical infrastructure. These attacks often begin with phishing emails, credential theft, or exploiting vulnerabilities in remote access solutions. Once inside the network, attackers deploy ransomware payloads, encrypt files, and demand payment in cryptocurrency. Some ransomware groups go beyond encryption by exfiltrating data and threatening to leak it publicly if the ransom is not paid. This double-extortion tactic increases pressure on victims and forces many organizations to comply with attackers' demands.

Another growing concern is supply chain attacks, where cybercriminals compromise third-party vendors, software providers, or service providers to infiltrate multiple organizations at once. These attacks exploit the interconnected nature of modern business operations, where companies rely on a vast network of external partners for cloud services, IT support, and software development. A single breach in a trusted supplier can have cascading effects across multiple organizations, leading to widespread data exposure and operational disruption. Notable incidents, such as the SolarWinds attack, have demonstrated how sophisticated adversaries can use supply chain vulnerabilities to conduct long-term espionage and data theft.

Cloud security has become a top priority as organizations migrate workloads to cloud environments. While cloud services offer scalability, flexibility, and cost efficiency, they also introduce new security challenges. Misconfigured cloud storage buckets, weak authentication controls, and improper access permissions have led to numerous high-profile data breaches. Attackers target cloud infrastructure by exploiting exposed APIs, stealing cloud credentials, and bypassing identity and access management policies. Additionally, multi-cloud and hybrid-cloud environments add complexity, making it difficult for security teams to maintain consistent security policies across different platforms. Organizations must adopt a Zero Trust approach, continuously verifying identities and enforcing least privilege access to mitigate cloud-based threats.

Insider threats have also evolved within the modern threat landscape. While malicious insiders remain a concern, unintentional insider threats have become equally damaging. Employees, contractors, and business partners may inadvertently expose sensitive data through misconfigurations, phishing scams, or poor security hygiene. Remote work has exacerbated these risks, as employees access corporate resources from personal devices, unsecured networks, and cloud-based collaboration tools. Security awareness training, continuous monitoring, and strict access controls are essential in mitigating insider threats and reducing the risk of accidental data exposure.

Cybercriminals increasingly leverage artificial intelligence (AI) and machine learning (ML) to enhance their attack capabilities. AI-driven phishing campaigns use natural language processing to generate convincing emails that bypass traditional spam filters. Deepfake technology allows attackers to create realistic voice and video impersonations, enabling business email compromise (BEC) and social engineering scams. Additionally, automated attack tools analyze vast amounts of stolen credentials, identify weak passwords, and execute large-scale credential stuffing attacks with minimal human intervention. Organizations must adopt AI-powered threat detection solutions to counter these advanced tactics and identify suspicious behavior in real time.

The widespread adoption of Internet of Things (IoT) devices has introduced new security risks. IoT devices, ranging from smart home appliances to industrial sensors, often lack robust security features, making them attractive targets for cybercriminals. Many IoT devices use default credentials, have outdated firmware, or lack encryption, allowing attackers to compromise them easily. Once infiltrated, these devices can be used as entry points into corporate networks, launch distributed denial-of-service (DDoS) attacks, or serve as part of botnets for large-scale cyberattacks. Organizations must implement strong authentication, network segmentation, and regular firmware updates to mitigate IoT-related threats.

Cyber espionage and nation-state attacks have become more prevalent, with state-sponsored groups targeting governments, corporations, and critical infrastructure. These attacks are highly sophisticated and often involve long-term infiltration, data exfiltration, and sabotage. Adversaries use advanced persistent threats (APTs) to maintain a stealthy presence within networks, leveraging zero-day vulnerabilities and custom malware to evade detection. In many cases, these attacks aim to steal intellectual property, disrupt economic stability, or gain a geopolitical advantage. Organizations operating in high-risk industries must implement advanced threat intelligence, endpoint detection and response (EDR), and multi-layered security measures to defend against state-sponsored threats.

The regulatory landscape has also evolved in response to the growing threat environment. Governments and industry regulators have introduced stringent data protection laws, compliance requirements, and cybersecurity standards to hold organizations accountable for security breaches. Regulations such as the General Data Protection Regulation (GDPR), the California Consumer Privacy Act (CCPA), and the Cybersecurity Maturity Model Certification (CMMC) mandate strict data protection practices, incident reporting, and risk assessments. Non-compliance with these regulations can result in significant financial penalties and reputational damage. Organizations must adopt a proactive security strategy to ensure compliance and protect customer data from unauthorized access.

With the increasing sophistication of cyber threats, security teams must take a proactive approach to threat detection and response. Traditional reactive security measures are no longer sufficient, as attackers constantly develop new techniques to bypass security controls. Organizations must invest in threat intelligence, behavioral analytics, and automated response mechanisms to stay ahead of cyber adversaries. Continuous monitoring, real-time threat correlation, and adaptive security measures are essential in defending against modern cyber threats. By understanding the evolving threat landscape, organizations can develop a resilient security posture, minimize the risk of breaches, and protect their digital assets from emerging attacks.

Identity and Access Management Fundamentals

Identity and Access Management (IAM) is a critical component of modern cybersecurity, ensuring that only authorized users have access to an organization's resources while keeping unauthorized individuals out. As businesses continue to adopt cloud services, remote work, and digital transformation initiatives, managing identities and controlling access has become more complex. A well-designed IAM framework helps organizations protect sensitive data, enforce security policies, and comply with regulatory requirements while maintaining operational efficiency.

At its core, IAM consists of two fundamental concepts: identity management and access control. Identity management involves the creation, maintenance, and lifecycle management of digital identities, ensuring that users, applications, and devices have the appropriate credentials and attributes. Access control, on the other hand, determines what resources each identity can access based on predefined policies, roles, and permissions. Together, these components form the foundation of a secure and efficient IT environment.

The IAM lifecycle begins with identity creation. When a new employee, contractor, or partner joins an organization, an identity is created within the IAM system. This process involves assigning a unique identifier, such as a username or employee ID, and associating it with relevant attributes, such as department, job role, and contact details. The identity is then linked to authentication credentials, such as passwords, biometrics, or cryptographic keys, which will be used to verify the user's legitimacy when accessing systems and applications.

Authentication is a critical aspect of IAM, ensuring that users are who they claim to be before granting access. Traditional authentication methods rely on passwords, but as attackers have become more adept at stealing credentials, stronger authentication mechanisms have been introduced. Multi-factor authentication (MFA) enhances security by requiring users to provide two or more authentication factors, such as a password and a one-time code sent to a mobile device. Adaptive authentication takes this concept further by assessing contextual information, such as the user's location, device, and behavior patterns, to determine the risk level of each login attempt.

Once authentication is successful, access control mechanisms determine what actions the user can perform within the system. Role-based access control (RBAC) is one of the most common access management models, assigning permissions based on predefined roles. For example, an HR manager may have access to employee records, while a software developer has access to code repositories. Attribute-based access control (ABAC) takes a more dynamic approach by evaluating user attributes, such as department, location, or security clearance, to grant or deny access in real time.

Privilege management plays a crucial role in IAM by restricting access to sensitive systems and preventing unauthorized privilege escalation. Privileged accounts, such as system administrators and database managers, have higher levels of access and pose a greater security risk if compromised. Privileged Access Management (PAM) solutions help secure these accounts by enforcing strict authentication requirements, limiting access based on just-in-time principles, and continuously monitoring privileged activities.

IAM also includes the management of user identities throughout their lifecycle. As employees change roles, transfer to different departments, or leave the organization, their access permissions must be updated accordingly. Failure to revoke access when an employee departs can lead to security vulnerabilities, as former employees may still have access to critical systems. Automated provisioning and deprovisioning processes help ensure that access rights are granted and revoked in a timely manner, reducing the risk of unauthorized access.

Federated identity management allows users to access multiple applications and services using a single set of credentials. This approach is particularly useful for organizations that use cloud services and third-party applications, as it reduces the need for users to manage multiple passwords. Single sign-on (SSO) is a common implementation of federated identity, allowing users to authenticate once and gain access to multiple systems without re-entering credentials. While SSO improves user experience and reduces password fatigue, it also introduces security challenges, as a compromised SSO account can grant attackers access to numerous resources. To mitigate this risk, organizations should implement strong authentication mechanisms and continuous monitoring of SSO sessions.

Identity governance ensures that IAM policies align with security and compliance requirements. Organizations must regularly audit access controls, review user privileges, and enforce least privilege principles to minimize security risks. Compliance regulations such as GDPR, HIPAA, and SOX require organizations to demonstrate proper identity management practices, including maintaining access logs, enforcing strong authentication policies, and conducting periodic access reviews. Identity governance solutions help automate these processes, providing visibility into user access and detecting anomalies that could indicate a security threat.

The growing adoption of cloud computing has introduced new IAM challenges, as organizations must manage identities across on-premises, hybrid, and multi-cloud environments. Cloud Identity and

Access Management (Cloud IAM) solutions provide centralized control over cloud-based identities, allowing organizations to enforce security policies consistently across different platforms. Cloud IAM solutions integrate with identity providers (IdPs) to enable secure authentication and authorization for cloud applications, reducing the complexity of managing multiple identity systems.

Identity threats, such as credential theft, account takeovers, and insider attacks, highlight the need for continuous monitoring and real-time threat detection. User behavior analytics (UBA) helps detect suspicious activities by analyzing access patterns, identifying deviations from normal behavior, and triggering alerts when potential security risks are detected. For example, if a user suddenly logs in from an unusual location, accesses sensitive data outside of normal business hours, or attempts to escalate privileges, security teams can investigate and take appropriate action.

IAM is a critical enabler of Zero Trust security, a model that assumes no user or system should be inherently trusted. Zero Trust principles require continuous verification of identities, strict enforcement of least privilege access, and constant monitoring of access activities. By implementing strong IAM practices, organizations can minimize attack surfaces, reduce the risk of unauthorized access, and enhance overall security posture.

The future of IAM will continue to evolve as new technologies and threats emerge. Advances in artificial intelligence and machine learning will enhance identity verification, fraud detection, and risk-based authentication. Decentralized identity solutions, powered by blockchain technology, may provide users with greater control over their personal data while improving security and privacy. As organizations navigate the complexities of digital transformation, a strong IAM framework will remain essential in protecting identities, securing access, and enabling seamless and secure user experiences.

Common Identity Threat Vectors

Identity threats have become one of the most significant security challenges for organizations, as attackers increasingly target user credentials and access controls to infiltrate systems. Traditional security models that focus solely on network perimeters are no longer sufficient, as identity-based attacks allow adversaries to bypass defenses and operate within trusted environments. By understanding the most common identity threat vectors, organizations can implement stronger defenses and reduce the risk of credential compromise, account takeovers, and unauthorized access.

One of the most widespread identity threat vectors is phishing, a social engineering attack designed to trick users into revealing their credentials. Phishing emails often appear to come from legitimate sources, such as banks, cloud service providers, or corporate IT departments, and lure victims into clicking malicious links. These links redirect users to fake login pages that closely resemble legitimate websites, where they unknowingly enter their usernames and passwords. More sophisticated phishing attacks, such as spear-phishing, specifically target high-value individuals within an organization, using personalized messages to increase the likelihood of success. Business email compromise (BEC) is another variation in which attackers impersonate executives or trusted partners to manipulate employees into transferring funds or sharing sensitive data.

Credential theft is another critical threat vector that attackers exploit to gain unauthorized access to systems. Cybercriminals use techniques such as keylogging, where malware secretly records keystrokes to capture usernames and passwords. They also deploy credential-stealing malware that extracts saved login credentials from web browsers, email clients, and password managers. Once attackers obtain valid credentials, they can use them to access corporate networks, cloud services, and other sensitive applications.

Credential stuffing has become a major issue due to the widespread reuse of passwords across multiple accounts. Attackers take advantage of previously breached credentials, testing them against various online services using automated tools. Because many users recycle passwords, successful credential stuffing attacks allow cybercriminals to gain access to banking accounts, corporate systems, and other critical services. Organizations that do not enforce multi-factor authentication (MFA) are particularly vulnerable to this type of attack, as attackers can log in using valid credentials without triggering additional security checks.

Password spraying is another attack method that exploits weak authentication practices. Instead of trying multiple passwords against a single account, attackers attempt a small number of commonly used passwords across many different accounts. This technique helps them avoid triggering account lockout mechanisms while increasing the chances of compromising accounts that use weak or default passwords. Organizations with large numbers of users, such as cloud service providers and educational institutions, are frequent targets of password spraying attacks.

Man-in-the-middle (MITM) attacks pose another serious risk to identity security by intercepting communications between users and legitimate authentication services. Attackers use techniques such as rogue Wi-Fi hotspots, DNS spoofing, or compromised network devices to eavesdrop on login credentials as they are transmitted. In cases where authentication data is not encrypted, attackers can easily capture usernames and passwords, allowing them to access accounts undetected. Even encrypted authentication methods are not immune, as attackers may use session hijacking techniques to take over an authenticated user's session without needing to steal their credentials directly.

Multi-factor authentication (MFA) was designed to mitigate identity threats by requiring additional verification beyond passwords. However, attackers have developed methods to bypass MFA protections. SIM swapping is a technique where cybercriminals trick or bribe mobile carriers into transferring a victim's phone number to a new SIM card under their control. Once they gain access to the victim's phone number, they can intercept MFA codes sent via SMS and use them to authenticate fraudulent logins. Other MFA-bypass techniques include man-in-the-browser (MITB) attacks, where malware injects malicious code into a user's browser to capture and replay MFA tokens in real time.

Session hijacking is another form of identity-based attack that targets active user sessions instead of credentials. Attackers steal session cookies or authentication tokens to impersonate a logged-in user without needing their username or password. These attacks are particularly effective against single sign-on (SSO) systems, where a single session token grants access to multiple applications. If an attacker obtains a valid session token, they can move laterally across systems without triggering additional authentication checks.

Privilege escalation is a tactic used by attackers to elevate their access privileges once inside a system. They start by compromising a low-level user account and then exploit misconfigurations, unpatched vulnerabilities, or weak access controls to gain higher-level privileges. Once they escalate to administrator or system-level privileges, they can disable security controls, modify access permissions, and exfiltrate sensitive data without restriction. Privileged Access Management (PAM) solutions help mitigate this risk by enforcing strict access controls and monitoring privileged account activities for suspicious behavior.

Insider threats also pose a significant risk to identity security, as employees, contractors, and business partners may misuse their access privileges for malicious purposes. Some insiders intentionally steal data for personal gain, while others are manipulated by external actors through coercion or financial incentives. Accidental insider threats are also common, where employees unknowingly expose credentials through phishing, weak password practices, or misconfigured access controls. Organizations must implement identity governance frameworks, enforce least privilege principles, and conduct regular access reviews to minimize insider risks.

Supply chain attacks have emerged as a growing identity threat vector, where attackers target third-party vendors and service providers to gain access to multiple organizations. By compromising an identity provider, software supplier, or cloud service, attackers can obtain privileged access to the systems of multiple clients. These attacks often involve inserting malicious code into trusted software updates, hijacking authentication mechanisms, or exploiting weak identity controls within supply chain networks. Organizations must conduct thorough security assessments of their vendors and enforce strong authentication and monitoring for third-party access.

Deepfake technology has introduced a new dimension to identity threats, enabling attackers to create realistic audio and video impersonations. Cybercriminals can use AI-generated deepfake voice or video calls to trick employees into authorizing fraudulent transactions or disclosing sensitive credentials. As this technology becomes more sophisticated, organizations must implement additional identity verification methods, such as behavioral biometrics and continuous authentication, to detect and prevent impersonation attacks.

The expanding use of cloud services has further complicated identity security, as organizations must manage identities across multiple environments. Misconfigurations in cloud identity and access management (IAM) settings can expose sensitive data and resources to unauthorized users. Attackers often scan cloud environments for exposed API keys, public storage buckets, and weak authentication policies to exploit misconfigured identity controls. Organizations must enforce strict IAM policies, use automated security monitoring, and implement Zero Trust principles to protect cloud-based identities.

As identity threats continue to evolve, security teams must stay ahead of emerging attack techniques by continuously monitoring for suspicious activity, enforcing strong authentication measures, and educating users on the risks of credential compromise. By adopting a proactive identity security strategy, organizations can reduce the likelihood of identity-based attacks and protect their critical assets from unauthorized access.

Credential Theft: Methods and Prevention

Credential theft has become one of the most effective and widely used techniques by cybercriminals to gain unauthorized access to systems, networks, and sensitive data. As organizations continue to rely on digital identities for authentication and authorization, stolen credentials provide attackers with a direct route into corporate environments without raising immediate suspicion. Once an attacker has obtained valid login credentials, they can move laterally within an organization, escalate privileges, and exfiltrate data without triggering traditional security defenses. Understanding the methods used to steal credentials and implementing effective prevention strategies is critical in reducing the risk of identity compromise.

One of the most common methods of credential theft is phishing, which relies on social engineering to trick users into revealing their login information. Attackers send deceptive emails that appear to be from trusted entities, such as banks, cloud service providers, or corporate IT departments, urging recipients to click on malicious links. These links direct users to fraudulent login pages that mimic legitimate websites, where they unknowingly enter their usernames and passwords. More sophisticated phishing attacks, such as spear-phishing, target specific individuals with personalized messages, increasing the likelihood of success. Business email compromise (BEC) attacks further exploit human trust by impersonating executives or business partners to manipulate employees into sharing sensitive credentials.

Keylogging is another widely used technique for credential theft, where attackers install malware that records keystrokes as victims type their usernames and passwords. Keyloggers are often delivered through malicious email attachments, compromised software downloads, or exploit kits that take advantage of unpatched vulnerabilities. Once installed, the malware silently captures login credentials and sends them to an attacker's command-and-control server. Because keyloggers operate at the system level, they can bypass traditional password security measures and compromise multiple accounts without the victim's knowledge.

Credential dumping is a more advanced technique used by attackers to extract stored credentials from compromised systems. Many operating systems and applications store login credentials in memory or credential databases, which can be exploited if proper security measures are not in place. Tools such as Mimikatz, LaZagne, and Metasploit allow attackers to retrieve hashed or plaintext credentials from Windows Security Accounts Manager (SAM), Local Security Authority Subsystem Service (LSASS), or browser-stored password databases. Once attackers obtain these credentials, they can use pass-the-hash (PtH) or pass-the-ticket (PtT) techniques to authenticate themselves without needing to crack passwords.

Man-in-the-middle (MITM) attacks provide another method for stealing credentials by intercepting network traffic between users and authentication services. Attackers set up rogue Wi-Fi hotspots, conduct DNS spoofing, or use ARP poisoning to capture login credentials as they are transmitted over the network. If authentication data is sent in plaintext or weakly encrypted, attackers can easily extract usernames and passwords. Even encrypted connections can be compromised through SSL stripping, where attackers downgrade secure HTTPS connections to unencrypted HTTP, allowing credentials to be intercepted in transit.

Credential theft is also facilitated through brute-force and credential stuffing attacks. Brute-force attacks involve systematically guessing passwords by trying different combinations until the correct one is found. While this method is time-consuming, attackers use automated tools to speed up the process, targeting weak or commonly used passwords. Credential stuffing, on the other hand, takes advantage of the fact that many users reuse passwords across multiple accounts. Attackers obtain lists of previously breached credentials and use automated scripts to test them against various online services, exploiting weak password reuse practices.

To combat credential theft, organizations must implement strong authentication mechanisms and enforce best security practices. Multi-factor authentication (MFA) is one of the most effective defenses, requiring users to verify their identity using an additional factor beyond their password. Even if an attacker steals a user's credentials, they will be unable to access the account without the secondary authentication factor, such as a one-time code, biometric verification, or hardware token. While MFA significantly reduces the risk of credential-based attacks, it must be implemented correctly, as attackers have developed methods to bypass weaker forms of MFA, such as SMS-based authentication.

Password hygiene plays a critical role in preventing credential theft. Organizations should enforce strong password policies, requiring users to create complex, unique passwords that are difficult to guess. Password managers can help users generate and store secure passwords without the need to remember them. Additionally, organizations should implement passwordless authentication solutions, such as biometric authentication or cryptographic-based authentication, to eliminate reliance on passwords altogether.

Continuous monitoring and behavioral analytics are essential in detecting and preventing credential theft. User behavior analytics

(UBA) can identify suspicious login attempts, such as logins from unusual locations, access attempts at odd hours, or multiple failed authentication attempts. Security teams can use anomaly detection to flag potential credential compromise and enforce additional security measures, such as requiring MFA reauthentication or temporarily locking accounts exhibiting unusual behavior.

Network security measures can further protect credentials from interception. Organizations should enforce end-to-end encryption for all authentication traffic, ensuring that login credentials are not transmitted in plaintext. Implementing Transport Layer Security (TLS) and HTTP Strict Transport Security (HSTS) prevents attackers from downgrading encrypted connections. Network segmentation and least privilege access policies limit the exposure of credential repositories, reducing the risk of credential dumping and lateral movement.

Privileged Access Management (PAM) is crucial in preventing attackers from escalating privileges using stolen credentials. PAM solutions enforce just-in-time access, requiring privileged users to request time-limited access to critical systems. By monitoring and auditing all privileged account activity, organizations can detect anomalies and respond to potential credential abuse before significant damage occurs.

Regular security awareness training helps employees recognize and avoid phishing attempts, social engineering attacks, and credential theft tactics. Simulated phishing campaigns and cybersecurity training programs reinforce security best practices, teaching users how to identify suspicious emails, verify the legitimacy of login requests, and report potential security threats. Organizations should also implement policies that discourage password reuse, encourage regular password updates, and require employees to use password managers for secure credential storage.

Threat intelligence and dark web monitoring can provide early warning signs of compromised credentials. Security teams can monitor underground forums, leaked credential databases, and breach notification services to identify if employee credentials have been exposed in data breaches. If compromised credentials are detected, organizations should enforce immediate password resets and investigate potential security breaches.

As attackers continue to refine their methods for stealing credentials, organizations must remain vigilant and adapt their security strategies accordingly. A multi-layered approach that combines strong authentication, behavioral analytics, network security, and user awareness training is essential in reducing the risk of credential theft. By continuously monitoring for suspicious activity, enforcing robust authentication mechanisms, and minimizing the attack surface, organizations can protect their users, data, and systems from credential-based attacks.

Multi-Factor Authentication: Strengths and Weaknesses

Multi-Factor Authentication (MFA) has become a cornerstone of modern cybersecurity, providing an additional layer of security beyond traditional password-based authentication. By requiring users to verify their identity using multiple factors, MFA significantly reduces the risk of unauthorized access due to stolen or compromised credentials. However, despite its strengths, MFA is not without weaknesses. Cybercriminals have developed methods to bypass or manipulate MFA protections, making it essential for organizations to understand both the benefits and limitations of this security measure.

The primary strength of MFA lies in its ability to enhance security by requiring users to provide at least two different forms of authentication. These authentication factors are generally categorized into three types: something the user knows (passwords, PINs, or security questions), something the user has (a smartphone, security token, or smart card), and something the user is (biometric data such as fingerprints, facial recognition, or retina scans). By combining multiple factors, MFA makes it significantly more difficult for attackers to gain unauthorized access, even if they have obtained a user's password.

One of the most common implementations of MFA is the use of time-based one-time passwords (TOTP), which are generated by authentication apps such as Google Authenticator, Microsoft Authenticator, or Authy. These codes expire within a short period, typically 30 to 60 seconds, making them difficult for attackers to reuse. Another common MFA method is SMS-based authentication, where users receive a one-time code via text message. While convenient, SMS-based MFA is vulnerable to interception methods such as SIM swapping, where attackers take control of a victim's phone number and receive their authentication codes.

Biometric authentication is another form of MFA that has gained popularity due to its convenience and security benefits. Fingerprint scanners, facial recognition, and iris scans are commonly used to verify identities in smartphones, laptops, and security systems. Unlike passwords or tokens, biometric data is unique to each individual and cannot be easily replicated. However, biometric authentication has its own security concerns. Biometric data, once compromised, cannot be changed like a password. Additionally, some biometric systems have been fooled by high-quality reproductions, such as fingerprint molds or deepfake-generated facial images.

One of the key strengths of MFA is its ability to mitigate the risks associated with password reuse and credential stuffing attacks. Many users reuse passwords across multiple accounts, making them vulnerable if one of their passwords is leaked in a data breach. MFA prevents attackers from accessing an account even if they have the correct password, as they would still need the second factor to complete the authentication process. This makes MFA an essential defense against credential-based attacks.

MFA is also effective against phishing attacks, which attempt to trick users into entering their login credentials on fraudulent websites. Even if an attacker successfully steals a user's password, they cannot log in without the second authentication factor. Some advanced phishing attacks, however, use real-time phishing proxies that capture MFA codes as they are entered, allowing attackers to bypass authentication in real time. This highlights the need for organizations to implement phishing-resistant MFA solutions, such as hardware-based security keys.

Despite its security benefits, MFA introduces several usability challenges. Some users find it inconvenient to enter an additional authentication factor, leading to frustration and resistance to adoption. If users lose access to their second factor—such as losing a phone with an authentication app or hardware token—they may be locked out of their accounts, requiring time-consuming recovery processes. Organizations must balance security and usability, providing backup authentication methods while ensuring they do not introduce new security risks.

Another challenge of MFA is its potential for implementation weaknesses. Poorly configured MFA systems can leave gaps that attackers can exploit. For example, some organizations allow users to bypass MFA through email-based authentication links, which can be compromised if an attacker gains access to the user's email account. Similarly, some MFA implementations allow users to "remember" devices for extended periods, reducing the effectiveness of the second authentication factor. Organizations must ensure that their MFA policies are robust, requiring re-authentication at appropriate intervals and disabling insecure fallback methods.

MFA solutions also require significant investment in infrastructure, training, and support. Organizations must deploy authentication servers, integrate MFA with existing applications, and educate employees on proper usage. Some legacy systems may not support modern MFA methods, requiring additional development efforts to enable compatibility. The cost and complexity of implementing MFA can be a barrier for small and mid-sized businesses, although cloud-based authentication services have made it more accessible.

Cybercriminals have also developed sophisticated techniques to bypass MFA, leveraging social engineering, malware, and technical exploits. Attackers may use pretexting to impersonate IT support and convince users to provide their MFA codes over the phone. In some cases, attackers deploy malware that intercepts authentication requests on infected devices, capturing MFA codes before they reach the intended destination. Some advanced attacks target weaknesses in the MFA process itself, such as leveraging session hijacking techniques to take control of authenticated user sessions without needing to reauthenticate.

One of the most effective ways to enhance MFA security is to implement phishing-resistant authentication methods. Hardware security keys, such as those using the FIDO2 standard, provide a high level of protection by requiring physical presence for authentication. Unlike one-time codes that can be intercepted or replayed, hardware security keys use cryptographic authentication that is resistant to phishing attacks. Organizations should prioritize the adoption of phishing-resistant MFA methods for high-risk users, such as executives, IT administrators, and financial personnel.

While MFA is a crucial security measure, it should be part of a broader identity security strategy rather than a standalone solution. Organizations must implement continuous monitoring, risk-based authentication, and behavioral analytics to detect anomalies and respond to potential threats in real time. Risk-based authentication dynamically adjusts authentication requirements based on contextual factors, such as user location, device fingerprinting, and login behavior. If an unusual login attempt is detected, the system may prompt for additional verification or block access entirely.

The effectiveness of MFA ultimately depends on how it is implemented and maintained. Organizations must ensure that users understand its importance, implement strong authentication policies, and regularly review their security posture to address emerging threats. As cybercriminals continue to develop new attack techniques, organizations must remain proactive in improving their authentication methods, adopting secure and resilient MFA solutions that protect against evolving identity threats.

Insider Threats: Detection and Mitigation

Insider threats pose a significant risk to organizations, as they involve individuals who already have legitimate access to sensitive systems and data. Unlike external cyber threats, which require attackers to bypass multiple layers of security, insider threats originate from within the organization. These threats can come from employees, contractors, business partners, or even former employees who retain access to critical resources. Insider threats are particularly dangerous because they often bypass traditional security measures, making them harder to detect and mitigate.

Insiders can pose a threat either intentionally or unintentionally. Malicious insiders deliberately exploit their access privileges to steal data, sabotage systems, or commit fraud for financial gain, revenge, or ideological reasons. These individuals may act alone or be recruited by external actors, such as cybercriminal organizations or nation-state attackers. Unintentional insiders, on the other hand, compromise security due to negligence, human error, or lack of awareness. An employee who falls for a phishing scam, misconfigures access controls, or shares sensitive data accidentally can create security vulnerabilities without intending to cause harm.

One of the primary challenges in detecting insider threats is distinguishing between normal and suspicious behavior. Employees and contractors regularly access critical systems as part of their job functions, making it difficult to determine when an action is legitimate or malicious. Traditional security tools that focus on perimeter defense, such as firewalls and intrusion detection systems, are often ineffective against insider threats because these individuals are already inside the network. Organizations must adopt a behavioral-based approach to insider threat detection, leveraging advanced analytics to identify anomalies and suspicious activity.

User and Entity Behavior Analytics (UEBA) plays a crucial role in detecting insider threats by establishing baselines of normal user behavior and flagging deviations. UEBA solutions analyze patterns in login activities, data access, file transfers, and privileged account usage to detect signs of potential insider threats. For example, if an employee who typically accesses customer data in small amounts suddenly begins downloading large volumes of sensitive files, this deviation could indicate malicious intent or a compromised account. By correlating multiple behavioral indicators, UEBA helps security teams detect insider threats before they escalate.

Monitoring privileged accounts is another critical aspect of insider threat detection. Employees with elevated access privileges, such as system administrators, database managers, and IT personnel, have the ability to make significant changes to systems and data. If these accounts are misused, they can cause severe damage, including data breaches, service disruptions, and financial losses. Privileged Access Management (PAM) solutions help mitigate insider threats by enforcing strict controls on privileged accounts. PAM solutions limit access to sensitive systems, enforce just-in-time privilege elevation, and require multi-factor authentication for high-risk actions.

Data Loss Prevention (DLP) technologies are essential for mitigating insider threats by monitoring and controlling the movement of sensitive data. DLP solutions prevent unauthorized data transfers by blocking suspicious file uploads, email attachments, and removable media usage. These tools also provide visibility into how employees handle sensitive data, enabling security teams to detect potential insider threats in real time. Organizations should implement DLP policies that restrict the unauthorized sharing of confidential information while allowing legitimate business processes to continue without disruption.

Insider threats are not limited to digital activities; physical security also plays a crucial role in mitigating risks. Employees with physical access to servers, data centers, and workstations can manipulate or steal sensitive information without triggering traditional cybersecurity defenses. Implementing access controls, surveillance systems, and biometric authentication for high-security areas helps prevent unauthorized physical access. Additionally, organizations should enforce policies that restrict the use of personal devices, external storage media, and unauthorized software installations within the corporate environment.

Security awareness training is a fundamental component of insider threat mitigation. Employees must understand the risks associated with insider threats and be educated on recognizing suspicious activities. Regular training sessions, phishing simulations, and security policy reinforcement help create a security-conscious workforce. Encouraging a culture of security awareness reduces the likelihood of unintentional insider threats and increases the chances of employees reporting suspicious behavior.

Organizations must also establish clear policies and procedures for managing insider threats. Implementing strict access controls based on the principle of least privilege ensures that employees only have access to the resources necessary for their job roles. Regular access reviews help identify and revoke unnecessary permissions, reducing the risk of privilege abuse. Organizations should also implement continuous monitoring of access logs, identifying unusual login attempts, unauthorized access to sensitive data, and failed authentication attempts that could indicate insider threat activity.

Psychological and behavioral indicators can also help identify potential insider threats. Employees who exhibit signs of dissatisfaction, financial distress, or conflicts with management may pose a higher risk of engaging in malicious activities. While organizations must respect employee privacy, HR and security teams can work together to monitor behavioral patterns that could indicate insider threat risks. Establishing anonymous reporting channels allows employees to report suspicious behavior without fear of retaliation, enabling security teams to investigate potential threats proactively.

Incident response planning is crucial for minimizing the impact of insider threats. Organizations should have predefined protocols for responding to suspected insider attacks, including isolating compromised accounts, conducting forensic investigations, and taking legal action if necessary. Security teams must collaborate with HR, legal, and compliance departments to ensure a coordinated response to insider threat incidents. Having a well-documented response plan ensures that organizations can act quickly and effectively when insider threats are detected.

The growing use of cloud services and remote work has further complicated insider threat mitigation. Employees accessing corporate resources from personal devices, unmanaged networks, and cloud applications create additional security challenges. Organizations must implement Zero Trust security principles, continuously verifying user identities and access requests before granting permissions. Cloud Access Security Brokers (CASBs) help monitor and enforce security policies across cloud environments, ensuring that data access is strictly controlled and monitored.

Organizations must take a proactive approach to insider threat detection and mitigation by combining advanced security technologies, employee training, strict access controls, and behavioral monitoring. By leveraging analytics, enforcing least privilege principles, and fostering a security-conscious culture, organizations can reduce the risk of insider threats and protect their critical assets from internal risks.

The Role of Privileged Access Management

Privileged Access Management (PAM) is a critical component of cybersecurity that focuses on securing, controlling, and monitoring access to privileged accounts and sensitive systems. Privileged accounts, such as system administrators, database managers, network engineers, and security teams, have elevated access rights that allow them to configure systems, manage data, and perform administrative tasks. Because these accounts have significant control over IT environments, they are prime targets for cybercriminals seeking to infiltrate organizations, steal data, and disrupt operations. Without proper oversight, compromised privileged accounts can lead to catastrophic security breaches, making PAM an essential defense mechanism in modern cybersecurity strategies.

One of the primary reasons PAM is crucial is the potential for privilege misuse, whether intentional or accidental. Malicious insiders can abuse privileged accounts to exfiltrate data, modify system configurations, or disrupt critical services. Even well-intentioned employees may make mistakes, such as misconfiguring security settings or sharing administrative credentials, which can expose systems to vulnerabilities. By implementing a robust PAM framework, organizations can enforce least privilege access, ensuring that users only have the permissions necessary to perform their specific job functions. This minimizes the risk of privilege abuse and limits the potential damage that compromised credentials can cause.

Cybercriminals actively target privileged accounts because they provide unrestricted access to critical systems. Attackers use various techniques to gain control of privileged credentials, including phishing, credential stuffing, keylogging, and credential dumping tools such as Mimikatz. Once attackers obtain privileged access, they can move laterally across networks, disable security controls, deploy malware, and exfiltrate sensitive data without triggering immediate alarms. PAM solutions help mitigate these risks by enforcing strong authentication measures, monitoring privileged activities, and restricting access based on risk levels.

One of the foundational principles of PAM is just-in-time (JIT) access, which limits the availability of privileged accounts to only when they are needed. Instead of granting users permanent administrative privileges, PAM solutions provide temporary, time-restricted access based on specific tasks or requests. This approach significantly reduces the attack surface by ensuring that privileged credentials are not constantly active and exposed to potential compromise. Additionally, JIT access helps organizations maintain better control over privileged actions by requiring approval processes and tracking all administrative activities.

Another critical component of PAM is credential vaulting, which securely stores and manages privileged account credentials. Instead of allowing users to know or manually enter administrative passwords, PAM solutions generate and rotate strong passwords automatically. When users need access to a privileged account, they authenticate through the PAM system, which grants them temporary access without exposing the actual credentials. This reduces the risk of credential theft, eliminates password reuse, and ensures that passwords are regularly updated to meet security policies.

Session monitoring and recording are essential features of PAM that provide visibility into privileged activities. PAM solutions can log all privileged user actions, including command executions, system modifications, and file access, creating an audit trail that helps security teams detect suspicious behavior. Some PAM solutions also offer real-time session monitoring, allowing security personnel to observe privileged activities as they occur and intervene if necessary. If an administrator starts executing unauthorized commands or accessing sensitive files outside of their typical job scope, security teams can take immediate action to investigate and mitigate potential threats.

Privileged Access Management also plays a vital role in enforcing multi-factor authentication (MFA) for privileged accounts. Requiring an additional layer of authentication beyond passwords significantly enhances security, making it more difficult for attackers to exploit stolen credentials. PAM solutions integrate with MFA providers to enforce strong authentication policies, ensuring that only authorized users can access privileged systems. Organizations should prioritize

MFA for all administrative accounts, especially those with access to critical infrastructure, financial data, and intellectual property.

The implementation of role-based access control (RBAC) and attribute-based access control (ABAC) further strengthens PAM strategies. RBAC assigns privileges based on predefined job roles, ensuring that users only have access to the systems necessary for their responsibilities. ABAC takes a more dynamic approach by considering contextual factors such as user location, device type, and risk level before granting access. By combining these access control models with PAM, organizations can enforce more granular security policies that adapt to evolving threats.

PAM solutions also help organizations comply with regulatory requirements and industry standards. Many compliance frameworks, including GDPR, HIPAA, SOX, and PCI DSS, mandate strict controls over privileged access to protect sensitive data and prevent unauthorized modifications. PAM solutions provide detailed access logs, session recordings, and audit trails that demonstrate compliance with these regulations. In the event of a security audit or investigation, organizations can use PAM reports to show how privileged access is managed, monitored, and secured.

As organizations continue to adopt cloud services, PAM strategies must extend beyond traditional on-premises environments to cloud-based systems. Cloud Privileged Access Management (Cloud PAM) solutions offer centralized control over privileged accounts across multi-cloud and hybrid environments, ensuring consistent security policies across different platforms. Cloud PAM solutions integrate with cloud identity providers, enforce least privilege access, and monitor privileged activities within cloud applications and infrastructure. Given the increasing use of cloud-native tools, such as Kubernetes and serverless computing, Cloud PAM is essential for securing dynamic and distributed IT environments.

Privileged access risks are not limited to human users; non-human accounts, such as service accounts, application accounts, and machine identities, also require strong security controls. Many organizations overlook the security of these accounts, which are often used to automate processes, integrate systems, and manage cloud workloads.

PAM solutions provide automated credential management for non-human accounts, ensuring that service account passwords are regularly rotated, encrypted, and restricted based on least privilege principles. By securing both human and machine identities, organizations can close security gaps that attackers frequently exploit.

To effectively implement PAM, organizations must adopt a continuous improvement approach, regularly reviewing and updating privileged access policies based on evolving threats. Security teams should conduct periodic access reviews to identify and remove unnecessary privileges, decommission unused privileged accounts, and enforce adaptive security measures. Conducting red team exercises and penetration testing can also help organizations identify weaknesses in their PAM implementations and address potential vulnerabilities before attackers can exploit them.

By enforcing strict controls over privileged accounts, organizations can significantly reduce their attack surface and limit the potential impact of security breaches. PAM solutions provide essential security capabilities, including just-in-time access, credential vaulting, session monitoring, multi-factor authentication, and cloud integration, all of which enhance overall cybersecurity posture. As cyber threats continue to evolve, implementing and maintaining a strong PAM framework is essential for protecting critical assets, ensuring compliance, and mitigating the risks associated with privileged access.

Zero Trust and Identity Security

Zero Trust has emerged as a fundamental security framework that challenges the traditional approach of assuming trust based on network location. In the past, organizations relied on perimeter-based security models, where once a user or device was inside the corporate network, they were granted broad access to resources. However, with the rise of cloud computing, remote work, and sophisticated cyber threats, this model has proven ineffective. Zero Trust shifts the security paradigm by enforcing a "never trust, always verify" approach, where every access request must be authenticated, authorized, and continuously validated based on risk factors.

Identity security is at the core of Zero Trust, as user and device authentication play a crucial role in enforcing strict access controls. Since traditional network boundaries no longer define security perimeters, organizations must ensure that only verified identities can access sensitive resources. This means that authentication should not be a one-time event but an ongoing process that continuously evaluates trust levels. Identity-centric security ensures that users, devices, and applications are granted access based on their current security posture, not just their initial credentials.

One of the foundational principles of Zero Trust is least privilege access. Users should only have access to the data and applications necessary for their role, and these permissions should be continuously reviewed and adjusted. Role-based access control (RBAC) and attribute-based access control (ABAC) play a key role in implementing least privilege by ensuring that access policies are dynamically enforced. Just-in-time (JIT) access further reduces risk by granting temporary access to resources only when needed, preventing long-term exposure of privileged credentials.

Multi-factor authentication (MFA) is a critical component of Zero Trust identity security, ensuring that authentication is not solely reliant on passwords. Passwords alone are highly vulnerable to phishing, credential stuffing, and brute-force attacks, making them an unreliable security measure. MFA strengthens authentication by requiring users to verify their identity through multiple factors, such as biometrics, hardware tokens, or one-time passcodes. However, attackers have developed methods to bypass MFA through social engineering and real-time phishing attacks, highlighting the need for phishing-resistant authentication methods, such as FIDO2 security keys or certificate-based authentication.

Continuous monitoring and risk-based authentication are essential for enforcing Zero Trust principles in identity security. Traditional authentication methods grant access based on initial login credentials, but Zero Trust requires ongoing evaluation of user behavior, device integrity, and contextual factors. Risk-based authentication adapts security measures based on factors such as geographic location, login patterns, device reputation, and historical user activity. If an access request appears suspicious—such as a login attempt from an unfamiliar location or an unusual time of day—the system can enforce additional security measures, such as requiring reauthentication or blocking access entirely.

Device security is another critical aspect of Zero Trust identity security. Since users access corporate resources from various devices, including personal laptops, mobile phones, and unmanaged endpoints, organizations must ensure that these devices meet security compliance requirements before granting access. Endpoint detection and response (EDR) solutions help monitor device activity and detect anomalies that could indicate a compromised system. Organizations can implement conditional access policies that restrict access based on device health, ensuring that only compliant and secure devices can connect to corporate resources.

The Zero Trust model also applies to workloads, applications, and APIs, ensuring that every entity in an IT environment is subject to strict authentication and authorization checks. Machine identities, such as service accounts, cloud workloads, and IoT devices, require the same level of scrutiny as human users. Attackers frequently target misconfigured APIs and weakly secured machine identities to move laterally within networks and escalate privileges. Implementing strong identity governance for both human and non-human identities is essential for maintaining a Zero Trust security posture.

Privileged Access Management (PAM) is tightly integrated with Zero Trust identity security, as privileged accounts represent a high-value target for attackers. Traditional security models often granted excessive privileges to users, allowing attackers to escalate access once they compromised an account. Zero Trust enforces strict control over privileged accounts by requiring just-in-time access, enforcing MFA, and monitoring all privileged activities. By continuously verifying privileged access requests, organizations can reduce the risk of insider threats and unauthorized privilege escalation.

The adoption of Zero Trust in cloud environments is particularly important, as cloud resources are frequently accessed from diverse locations and devices. Cloud Identity and Access Management (Cloud IAM) solutions provide centralized control over identity security in cloud environments, ensuring that access policies are consistently enforced across multiple platforms. Cloud-native security solutions, such as Cloud Access Security Brokers (CASBs) and Security Service Edge (SSE), help monitor and enforce Zero Trust principles in cloud applications, preventing unauthorized access and data exposure.

One of the challenges of implementing Zero Trust is balancing security with user experience. Strict access controls and continuous verification can introduce friction for users, leading to decreased productivity and frustration. Organizations must adopt adaptive authentication strategies that intelligently adjust security requirements based on contextual risk factors. By leveraging artificial intelligence and machine learning, security systems can analyze user behavior and determine the appropriate level of authentication needed for each request, minimizing disruptions while maintaining strong security.

Zero Trust security models also require strong identity governance frameworks to ensure that access policies remain up to date. Organizations must conduct regular access reviews, remove unnecessary privileges, and enforce identity lifecycle management processes. Automating identity governance through identity access management (IAM) solutions helps organizations maintain compliance with regulatory requirements while reducing administrative overhead.

Threat intelligence and real-time security analytics enhance Zero Trust identity security by providing insights into emerging threats and suspicious activities. Security teams can leverage advanced analytics to detect compromised accounts, insider threats, and anomalous behaviors that may indicate an ongoing attack. Integrating Zero Trust identity security with Security Information and Event Management (SIEM) and Extended Detection and Response (XDR) platforms provides a comprehensive view of security risks across an organization.

As organizations adopt Zero Trust principles, security culture and employee awareness play a crucial role in ensuring effective implementation. Employees must be educated on the importance of identity security, recognizing phishing attempts, and following best practices for secure authentication. Implementing security awareness training programs and phishing simulations helps reinforce Zero Trust principles and reduces the risk of social engineering attacks.

Zero Trust identity security is not a one-time implementation but an ongoing process that requires continuous adaptation to evolving threats. Organizations must regularly evaluate their security posture, update access policies, and leverage emerging technologies to enhance identity protection. By adopting a Zero Trust approach to identity security, organizations can minimize the risk of identity-based attacks, enforce least privilege access, and create a resilient security framework that protects users, data, and systems from both internal and external threats.

User Behavior Analytics for Identity Protection

User Behavior Analytics (UBA) has become an essential tool in identity protection, helping organizations detect and mitigate security threats by analyzing patterns of user activity. Traditional security measures focus on static rules, such as password policies and access controls, but these methods often fail to detect sophisticated attacks that involve credential compromise, insider threats, and privilege abuse. UBA enhances security by continuously monitoring user behavior, identifying anomalies, and flagging suspicious activity that may indicate a potential security breach.

Identity-based attacks have become increasingly sophisticated, making it difficult to distinguish between legitimate users and attackers who have stolen credentials. Cybercriminals use techniques such as phishing, credential stuffing, and social engineering to obtain valid login credentials, allowing them to bypass traditional authentication mechanisms. Once inside an organization's network, attackers often behave like legitimate users, gradually escalating privileges and exfiltrating data without triggering security alerts. UBA helps address this challenge by establishing behavioral baselines for each user and detecting deviations from normal activity.

The core principle of UBA is that every user has a unique behavioral pattern based on their daily interactions with corporate systems. These patterns include login times, access locations, frequently used applications, data access frequency, and typical file transfer activities. By analyzing these patterns over time, UBA systems can create a behavioral profile for each user, allowing security teams to identify anomalies that may indicate a potential security threat. For example, if an employee who typically logs in from New York suddenly accesses systems from an IP address in a foreign country, this could indicate a compromised account.

UBA uses advanced machine learning algorithms and statistical models to detect behavioral anomalies. Instead of relying on predefined rules, machine learning continuously adapts to changing user behaviors, improving its ability to differentiate between normal and suspicious activities. For instance, if an employee typically downloads small files for routine tasks but suddenly starts transferring large volumes of sensitive data, the UBA system can flag this as a potential data exfiltration attempt. Unlike traditional security systems that generate alerts based on fixed thresholds, UBA dynamically adjusts its detection models based on evolving user behaviors.

One of the key advantages of UBA is its ability to detect insider threats. While most security solutions focus on external threats, insider threats can be just as damaging, if not more so. Malicious insiders, such as disgruntled employees or corporate spies, may abuse their access privileges to steal data, modify critical systems, or disrupt business operations. Even well-intentioned employees can inadvertently expose sensitive data by falling for phishing scams or mishandling credentials. UBA helps mitigate these risks by continuously monitoring user activity and identifying behavior that deviates from established norms.

UBA can also detect privilege escalation attempts, where an attacker or insider tries to gain higher levels of access than they are authorized to have. If an employee who normally accesses customer support databases suddenly attempts to access confidential financial records or executive emails, the UBA system can generate an alert for further investigation. By analyzing access requests in real-time, UBA helps prevent unauthorized privilege escalation before it leads to a security incident.

Another critical application of UBA is in detecting compromised accounts. Attackers who obtain stolen credentials often try to blend in with normal user activity to avoid detection. However, even if they use valid credentials, their behavior is unlikely to match that of the legitimate account owner. UBA can identify subtle inconsistencies, such as logging in at unusual hours, accessing rarely used applications, or attempting unauthorized transactions. By correlating these anomalies with other security signals, such as failed login attempts or unusual file transfers, UBA provides a more comprehensive approach to detecting account takeovers.

UBA is also valuable in preventing lateral movement within an organization's network. Once an attacker gains initial access, they typically attempt to move laterally, exploring different systems and escalating privileges to reach their final target. Traditional security tools may not detect this activity if it appears to come from an authenticated user. However, UBA can identify suspicious patterns, such as an employee accessing multiple systems they have never used before or attempting to authenticate from multiple locations within a short time. These signals can help security teams stop attackers before they can cause significant damage.

Implementing UBA effectively requires integration with existing security infrastructure, such as Identity and Access Management (IAM) systems, Security Information and Event Management (SIEM) platforms, and endpoint detection solutions. By aggregating data from multiple sources, UBA can provide a holistic view of user activity and correlate behavioral anomalies with other security indicators. Organizations should also implement automated response mechanisms that take action when high-risk behaviors are detected. For example, if UBA detects an unauthorized attempt to access sensitive financial data, it can trigger an automated response to require multi-factor authentication (MFA) or temporarily lock the account until further verification is performed.

Despite its many advantages, UBA is not without challenges. One of the primary concerns is the risk of false positives, where legitimate user behavior is mistakenly classified as suspicious. For instance, if an employee travels frequently for business, their logins from different locations may trigger alerts even though they are legitimate. To address this, UBA systems must be fine-tuned to account for variations in user behavior while minimizing unnecessary alerts. Security teams should also establish clear procedures for investigating UBA alerts, ensuring that potential threats are assessed accurately before taking action.

Privacy considerations are another challenge when deploying UBA. Because UBA involves continuous monitoring of user activity, organizations must implement it in a way that respects employee privacy while maintaining security. Transparent communication with employees about the purpose of UBA and how data is used can help build trust and reduce concerns about surveillance. Organizations should also follow data protection regulations, such as GDPR and CCPA, ensuring that user behavior data is handled responsibly and securely.

As identity-based threats continue to evolve, UBA will play an increasingly important role in protecting organizations from cyber risks. The combination of machine learning, behavioral analytics, and automated response mechanisms makes UBA a powerful tool for detecting compromised accounts, insider threats, and privilege abuse. By continuously analyzing user activity and adapting to emerging threats, UBA enhances identity protection and strengthens overall security posture. Organizations that integrate UBA into their security strategy will be better equipped to detect and mitigate threats before they escalate into full-scale breaches.

Threat Intelligence and Identity Protection

Threat intelligence has become an essential component of modern cybersecurity, providing organizations with actionable insights into emerging threats, attack techniques, and adversary behaviors. As identity-based attacks continue to rise, integrating threat intelligence into identity protection strategies allows security teams to detect, prevent, and respond to threats more effectively. By leveraging real-time data on malicious activities, stolen credentials, and evolving attack patterns, organizations can strengthen their defenses and mitigate identity-related risks before they escalate into full-scale security breaches.

Identity threats have evolved significantly in recent years, with cybercriminals increasingly targeting user credentials, privileged accounts, and authentication mechanisms. Traditional security measures, such as firewalls and antivirus software, are no longer sufficient to prevent identity-based attacks, as many of these threats exploit legitimate login credentials rather than relying on malware or direct system exploitation. Threat intelligence provides organizations with the ability to anticipate these attacks by analyzing global threat trends, monitoring dark web activity, and identifying compromised credentials before they are used in an attack.

One of the most critical applications of threat intelligence in identity protection is the detection of stolen credentials. Cybercriminals frequently trade stolen usernames, passwords, and authentication tokens on underground forums and dark web marketplaces. Threat intelligence feeds aggregate data from these sources, allowing organizations to identify whether their employees' credentials have been compromised in previous breaches. If a match is found, organizations can take proactive measures such as forcing password resets, enabling multi-factor authentication (MFA), or blocking access from suspicious locations. By continuously monitoring for credential leaks, organizations can prevent unauthorized access before attackers have the chance to exploit compromised accounts.

Threat intelligence also plays a crucial role in detecting phishing campaigns, which remain one of the most effective methods for stealing credentials. Cybercriminals use sophisticated phishing tactics to impersonate legitimate organizations, tricking users into revealing their login information. Advanced threat intelligence platforms track phishing domains, malicious URLs, and email-based scams in real time, enabling security teams to block phishing attempts before they reach end users. Integrating threat intelligence with email security gateways, endpoint protection solutions, and user awareness training helps reduce the success rate of phishing attacks and strengthens identity protection.

Another key aspect of threat intelligence in identity security is the detection of anomalous authentication attempts. Cybercriminals often test stolen credentials using automated tools in credential stuffing and brute-force attacks. Threat intelligence platforms collect data on suspicious IP addresses, botnet activity, and login patterns associated with credential abuse. By integrating this intelligence into identity and access management (IAM) solutions, organizations can detect login attempts from known malicious sources and implement additional security controls, such as requiring MFA or blocking access from high-risk geolocations.

Threat intelligence also enhances insider threat detection by providing insights into emerging attack techniques and behavioral indicators of compromise. While many insider threats originate from employees or contractors with legitimate access, some are influenced or recruited by external adversaries. Threat intelligence helps organizations identify patterns of insider-related risks, such as unauthorized data transfers, privilege escalation attempts, or access to sensitive information outside of normal work hours. By correlating internal security events with external threat intelligence, organizations can better identify potential insider threats and take proactive measures to mitigate risks.

Security teams can further strengthen identity protection by leveraging threat intelligence in the context of behavioral analytics. User and Entity Behavior Analytics (UEBA) systems can integrate threat intelligence feeds to refine risk scoring models and improve anomaly detection. For example, if a user attempts to log in from an IP address associated with a known threat actor, the UEBA system can flag the activity as high risk and enforce additional authentication steps. This combination of internal monitoring and external threat intelligence provides a more comprehensive approach to identity security.

Threat intelligence also supports incident response efforts by providing security teams with critical context about ongoing attacks. When an identity-related breach occurs, security analysts can use threat intelligence to determine the origin of the attack, identify whether similar incidents have been reported globally, and assess the tactics, techniques, and procedures (TTPs) used by the attackers. This information helps organizations develop effective containment strategies, prevent further compromise, and strengthen their defenses against similar attacks in the future.

As organizations adopt cloud-based identity management solutions, threat intelligence becomes even more critical in securing cloud environments. Cybercriminals frequently target cloud authentication mechanisms, including federated identity services, single sign-on (SSO) platforms, and API keys. Threat intelligence provides security teams with real-time insights into cloud-based attack trends, allowing them to implement proactive security measures such as enforcing least privilege access, monitoring for unusual login behaviors, and detecting API abuse attempts.

One of the challenges of implementing threat intelligence for identity protection is the need to filter and analyze large volumes of data. Not all threat intelligence is relevant to every organization, and security teams must focus on actionable intelligence that directly impacts their identity security posture. Organizations should prioritize threat intelligence sources that provide real-time updates on credential leaks, phishing campaigns, malicious IP addresses, and adversary behaviors related to identity attacks. Automated threat intelligence platforms can help streamline this process by integrating with IAM, SIEM (Security Information and Event Management), and XDR (Extended Detection and Response) systems.

Collaboration and information sharing also play a crucial role in maximizing the effectiveness of threat intelligence for identity protection. Many cybersecurity frameworks encourage organizations to participate in threat intelligence-sharing initiatives, such as Information Sharing and Analysis Centers (ISACs) and government-backed cyber threat intelligence programs. By sharing identity-related threat intelligence across industries and sectors, organizations can collectively improve their defenses and respond more effectively to emerging threats.

The adoption of artificial intelligence and machine learning further enhances the capabilities of threat intelligence in identity protection. AI-driven threat intelligence platforms can analyze vast amounts of threat data, identify patterns, and predict emerging attack trends with greater accuracy. Machine learning models can also improve automated detection and response mechanisms, allowing organizations to identify and mitigate identity threats in real time without manual intervention. As cyber threats continue to evolve, AI-powered threat intelligence will play an increasingly important role in defending against sophisticated identity-based attacks.

As organizations refine their security strategies, integrating threat intelligence with identity protection frameworks is no longer optional—it is a necessity. The ability to proactively identify and mitigate identity threats based on real-time intelligence provides a significant advantage in preventing account takeovers, credential abuse, and insider threats. By leveraging the latest threat intelligence, organizations can stay ahead of cybercriminals, strengthen authentication mechanisms, and protect user identities in an increasingly hostile digital landscape.

Cloud Identity Threats and Defenses

As organizations continue migrating to cloud environments, identity security has become a primary concern. Unlike traditional on-premises systems, where security controls are centralized within a corporate network, cloud services operate in distributed environments with multiple access points. This shift introduces new identity threats that attackers can exploit to gain unauthorized access, compromise data, and escalate privileges. Without robust identity security measures, cloud environments become prime targets for cybercriminals seeking to exploit misconfigurations, stolen credentials, and weak authentication mechanisms. Understanding the key cloud identity threats and implementing effective defenses is crucial for maintaining a secure cloud ecosystem.

One of the most prevalent cloud identity threats is credential theft. Cloud-based services rely heavily on usernames and passwords for authentication, making them attractive targets for attackers. Cybercriminals use various methods to steal credentials, including phishing attacks, credential stuffing, and brute-force attempts. Once an attacker gains access to valid cloud credentials, they can move laterally within the environment, escalate privileges, and exfiltrate sensitive data without raising immediate alarms. The widespread use of password reuse across multiple accounts further exacerbates this issue, as attackers can use credentials from one breached service to access other cloud-based applications.

Misconfigured identity and access management (IAM) settings represent another significant risk in cloud environments. Many cloud security breaches occur due to improperly configured IAM policies that grant excessive privileges or expose critical resources to unauthorized users. For example, an organization may mistakenly configure a cloud storage bucket to be publicly accessible, allowing attackers to exfiltrate sensitive data without needing authentication. Similarly, weak role-based access control (RBAC) implementations can lead to privilege escalation, where a compromised low-level account is used to gain administrative access to cloud resources. Organizations that fail to regularly audit and refine their IAM policies risk leaving their cloud environments exposed to potential attacks.

Insufficient multi-factor authentication (MFA) adoption is another common weakness in cloud identity security. While MFA significantly enhances security by requiring an additional authentication factor beyond passwords, many organizations still fail to enforce MFA for all users. Attackers have also developed techniques to bypass weak MFA implementations, such as SIM swapping attacks, where they hijack a victim's mobile number to intercept one-time passcodes. Additionally, real-time phishing attacks use proxy-based techniques to capture both passwords and MFA codes, allowing attackers to authenticate as legitimate users. Organizations that rely solely on SMS-based MFA should consider adopting stronger authentication methods, such as FIDO2 security keys or app-based push notifications, to mitigate these risks.

Session hijacking poses another identity threat in cloud environments. Attackers can steal authentication tokens and session cookies from users to gain unauthorized access to cloud services without needing login credentials. This is particularly dangerous in cloud applications that do not enforce session expiration or re-authentication mechanisms. Once an attacker obtains a valid session token, they can impersonate the legitimate user and access cloud resources without detection. Secure token management, regular session expiration policies, and endpoint security measures help mitigate the risks associated with session hijacking.

API security is a growing concern in cloud identity protection, as cloud applications increasingly rely on APIs for communication between services. Attackers target poorly secured APIs to bypass authentication controls, extract sensitive data, and manipulate cloud resources. Common API security flaws include weak authentication mechanisms, exposed API keys, and lack of rate limiting. Attackers can exploit these weaknesses to conduct automated attacks, such as credential stuffing, data scraping, and privilege escalation. Organizations should implement strong API authentication, such as OAuth 2.0 and JWT-based tokens, enforce least privilege access for API permissions, and monitor API activity for suspicious behavior.

The rise of cloud-based identity federation and single sign-on (SSO) solutions introduces new security challenges. While SSO enhances user convenience by allowing seamless access across multiple cloud applications, it also creates a single point of failure if compromised. If an attacker gains control of an SSO account, they can access all linked applications without needing to bypass individual authentication mechanisms. To mitigate this risk, organizations should enforce adaptive authentication policies that assess contextual risk factors, such as login location, device fingerprinting, and behavioral patterns. Implementing continuous authentication mechanisms ensures that user identities are verified throughout their sessions, reducing the risk of SSO compromise.

Privilege escalation attacks remain a significant threat in cloud environments, as attackers seek to elevate their access privileges to gain control over critical resources. Misconfigured IAM policies, excessive permissions, and poorly secured service accounts provide attackers with opportunities to escalate their privileges once inside a cloud environment. Attackers often exploit identity trust relationships between cloud services to gain additional access beyond their initial foothold. Organizations should enforce least privilege access, regularly review IAM policies, and implement automated identity governance solutions to detect and prevent privilege escalation attempts.

To defend against cloud identity threats, organizations must implement a Zero Trust security model, where no user or device is inherently trusted. Zero Trust principles require continuous authentication, least privilege access, and strict access controls for all cloud resources. Instead of relying on traditional perimeter-based security, Zero Trust enforces identity verification at every stage of access. Organizations should adopt continuous monitoring solutions that analyze user behavior, detect anomalies, and trigger automated responses when suspicious activity is detected.

Identity threat detection and response (ITDR) solutions provide an additional layer of security by continuously monitoring identity-related events in cloud environments. ITDR platforms integrate with IAM solutions, security information and event management (SIEM) systems, and extended detection and response (XDR) platforms to provide real-time visibility into identity threats. By analyzing authentication logs, access patterns, and privilege escalation attempts, ITDR solutions help organizations detect identity compromises and take proactive security measures.

Security awareness training plays a crucial role in mitigating cloud identity threats by educating employees on best practices for credential security, phishing prevention, and secure authentication. Organizations should implement regular training programs to ensure that users understand the risks associated with cloud identity attacks and how to recognize social engineering attempts. Encouraging the use of password managers, enforcing strong password policies, and conducting phishing simulations can help reduce the risk of credential compromise.

As cloud adoption continues to grow, organizations must remain vigilant in securing their identity infrastructure. By implementing strong authentication mechanisms, enforcing least privilege access, continuously monitoring identity activity, and integrating threat intelligence, organizations can build a resilient identity security framework. Cloud identity security should be an ongoing priority, with regular assessments, policy updates, and security enhancements to adapt to emerging threats. By taking a proactive approach to cloud identity protection, organizations can mitigate risks and safeguard their cloud environments from identity-based attacks.

Identity Compromise in Hybrid Environments

Hybrid environments, where organizations operate a mix of on-premises and cloud-based infrastructure, present unique security challenges, particularly when it comes to identity protection. As businesses transition from traditional IT architectures to cloud-based solutions, they must ensure seamless yet secure identity and access management across both environments. However, this complexity often introduces vulnerabilities that attackers can exploit to compromise identities, gain unauthorized access, and move laterally across systems. Identity compromise in hybrid environments is a growing concern, as attackers leverage weaknesses in identity synchronization, misconfigured authentication policies, and gaps in visibility to infiltrate corporate networks.

One of the primary risks in hybrid environments is the synchronization of identities between on-premises Active Directory (AD) and cloud identity providers such as Azure Active Directory (Azure AD), Okta, or Google Workspace. Many organizations maintain a hybrid identity model where user credentials and access policies are synchronized across both environments. If an attacker gains control of an on-premises identity—through phishing, credential theft, or privilege escalation—they may be able to extend that compromise to cloud resources if identity synchronization is not properly secured. Weak password policies, unprotected synchronization channels, and misconfigured directory federation settings can all increase the risk of hybrid identity compromise.

Another major threat vector in hybrid environments is misconfigured Single Sign-On (SSO) and authentication mechanisms. SSO allows users to access multiple systems with a single set of credentials, improving usability but also creating a single point of failure. If an attacker compromises an SSO-enabled account, they can gain access to both on-premises and cloud applications without needing to bypass separate authentication barriers. Organizations must enforce strong authentication policies, such as multi-factor authentication (MFA) and conditional access controls, to reduce the risk of SSO-related identity compromise.

Lateral movement between hybrid systems is a key tactic used by attackers once they have gained initial access. Many hybrid environments have interconnected authentication mechanisms, where an attacker who compromises an on-premises account can leverage trust relationships to access cloud resources. Techniques such as pass-the-hash (PtH), pass-the-ticket (PtT), and golden ticket attacks allow adversaries to exploit Kerberos authentication and move between on-premises and cloud systems without triggering standard security alerts. Implementing strong privileged access management (PAM) controls, enforcing least privilege access, and continuously monitoring authentication logs can help detect and prevent such lateral movement.

Hybrid environments also introduce risks associated with service accounts and machine identities. Many organizations use automated scripts, third-party integrations, and API connections that require persistent credentials to function. If these credentials are hardcoded in configuration files, stored in plaintext, or poorly secured, attackers can exploit them to gain access to both on-premises and cloud-based systems. Service accounts often have elevated privileges and are rarely monitored, making them attractive targets for attackers. Organizations should enforce strict credential management policies, use secrets management solutions, and regularly audit service account activity to mitigate these risks.

Another challenge in hybrid environments is visibility and monitoring. Security teams must correlate identity-related events across both on-premises and cloud environments to detect suspicious activity effectively. However, many organizations lack unified logging and monitoring tools that provide comprehensive visibility into hybrid identity threats. Attackers take advantage of these blind spots by using techniques such as cloud account takeover, privilege escalation, and token hijacking. Implementing a Security Information and Event Management (SIEM) solution that aggregates identity logs from both environments can help detect anomalies and provide early warning of identity compromise.

Multi-factor authentication (MFA) plays a critical role in securing hybrid identities, but its effectiveness depends on proper implementation. Some organizations enforce MFA only for cloud-based applications while leaving on-premises authentication vulnerable. This inconsistency creates an opportunity for attackers to exploit weaker authentication mechanisms to gain a foothold in the environment. MFA should be enforced consistently across all identity platforms, including on-premises Active Directory, VPN access, cloud applications, and privileged accounts. Additionally, organizations should adopt phishing-resistant authentication methods, such as hardware security keys and certificate-based authentication, to counter evolving attack techniques.

Misconfigurations in hybrid identity governance are another major cause of identity compromise. Organizations that fail to enforce least privilege access across both environments risk overprivileged accounts becoming targets for attackers. Security teams must conduct regular access reviews to identify and revoke unnecessary permissions, ensuring that users have only the access they need for their specific roles. Automated identity governance solutions can help enforce these policies by continuously monitoring and adjusting access rights based on real-time risk assessments.

The growing use of cloud-based collaboration tools, such as Microsoft Teams, Slack, and Google Drive, introduces additional identity risks in hybrid environments. Many of these applications integrate with on-premises directories, allowing users to authenticate with corporate credentials. If an attacker compromises a user account through phishing or social engineering, they may gain access to sensitive company data stored in cloud applications. Organizations must implement data loss prevention (DLP) solutions and enforce strict sharing policies to prevent unauthorized data exposure.

Attackers also exploit hybrid environments through shadow IT, where employees use unauthorized cloud services and applications without IT oversight. When users create accounts on external cloud platforms using corporate email addresses, these unmanaged identities can become security risks. If an attacker gains control of a shadow IT account, they may use it to impersonate an employee, distribute malware, or conduct phishing attacks. Organizations should implement cloud access security brokers (CASBs) to detect and manage shadow IT activities while educating employees on secure cloud usage policies.

Incident response for identity compromise in hybrid environments requires a coordinated approach that spans both on-premises and cloud security teams. Organizations must establish clear protocols for investigating identity breaches, containing compromised accounts, and restoring secure access. Automated response mechanisms, such as risk-based authentication and adaptive access controls, can help mitigate ongoing threats by dynamically adjusting authentication requirements based on detected anomalies. Additionally, conducting regular tabletop exercises and penetration tests can help security teams prepare for real-world identity-based attacks.

Hybrid environments require a security-first approach to identity management, where authentication, access control, and monitoring are consistently enforced across all platforms. Organizations must continuously assess their hybrid identity security posture, implementing best practices such as strong authentication, least privilege access, real-time monitoring, and automated threat detection. By addressing identity vulnerabilities proactively, businesses can reduce the risk of compromise and ensure that their hybrid environments remain secure against evolving threats.

Social Engineering and Identity Fraud

Social engineering and identity fraud have become two of the most effective techniques used by cybercriminals to manipulate individuals into disclosing sensitive information, compromising their identities, and granting unauthorized access to systems. Unlike traditional cyberattacks that rely on exploiting technical vulnerabilities, social engineering attacks target human psychology, exploiting trust, curiosity, fear, or urgency to deceive victims. Once attackers obtain personal or corporate identity information, they can use it to commit fraud, impersonate legitimate users, or gain access to restricted systems. As identity-based threats continue to rise, understanding how social engineering tactics work and how to defend against them is crucial for organizations and individuals alike.

One of the most common forms of social engineering is phishing, where attackers send deceptive emails that appear to come from trusted sources, such as banks, government agencies, or corporate IT departments. These emails often contain urgent messages prompting the recipient to click on a malicious link, download a compromised attachment, or enter their login credentials on a fake website. The goal is to trick the victim into revealing sensitive identity information, such as usernames, passwords, or credit card details. More sophisticated phishing techniques, such as spear-phishing, involve highly targeted attacks tailored to specific individuals or organizations, making them more difficult to detect. Attackers gather information about their targets from social media, company websites, and data breaches to craft convincing messages that increase the likelihood of success.

Another dangerous social engineering tactic is pretexting, where attackers create a fabricated scenario to convince victims to provide sensitive information or perform certain actions. In these attacks, cybercriminals pose as authority figures, such as IT administrators, HR personnel, or law enforcement officers, and request confidential details under the guise of routine verification or emergency response. For example, an attacker may call an employee pretending to be from the IT department and claim that their account has been compromised. Under this pretext, they instruct the employee to provide their credentials or approve a fraudulent multi-factor authentication (MFA) request. Because pretexting relies on psychological manipulation rather than technical exploits, it can be highly effective in bypassing security controls.

Identity fraud occurs when cybercriminals use stolen personal or corporate identity information to impersonate individuals for financial gain or unauthorized access. Once attackers obtain personally identifiable information (PII), such as social security numbers, birth dates, or passport details, they can open fraudulent bank accounts, apply for credit cards, or commit tax fraud under a victim's identity. In corporate environments, identity fraud enables attackers to impersonate executives, employees, or vendors to carry out business email compromise (BEC) attacks. These attacks often involve requesting fraudulent wire transfers, redirecting payroll deposits, or gaining access to sensitive corporate resources. Because attackers use real identity information, detecting and preventing identity fraud can be challenging without advanced identity verification measures.

Vishing (voice phishing) and smishing (SMS phishing) are extensions of traditional phishing attacks that use phone calls or text messages instead of emails to manipulate victims. In vishing attacks, cybercriminals call victims pretending to be customer support representatives, government officials, or financial institutions and use persuasion techniques to extract identity information. Smishing attacks, on the other hand, involve fraudulent text messages containing malicious links or urgent requests, such as fake bank alerts requiring users to verify their credentials. As mobile communication becomes more widely used, attackers are increasingly leveraging vishing and smishing techniques to bypass email security filters and target victims directly.

Attackers also exploit social media platforms to gather intelligence on potential victims and execute identity fraud schemes. Many users unknowingly share personal details, such as their full names, locations, job titles, and travel plans, which attackers can use to craft convincing social engineering attacks. For example, an attacker who knows that an employee recently attended a corporate event may send a follow-up email posing as a colleague or event organizer to request login credentials. Social media impersonation is another form of identity fraud where attackers create fake profiles using stolen photos and identity details to deceive contacts, spread malware, or conduct financial scams.

Deepfake technology has further amplified the risks of social engineering and identity fraud by enabling attackers to create realistic audio and video impersonations. With advancements in artificial intelligence (AI), cybercriminals can generate deepfake videos or voice recordings that mimic real individuals with high accuracy. This has led to sophisticated fraud schemes where attackers impersonate company executives in video calls or voice messages to authorize financial transactions or disclose sensitive information. As deepfake technology becomes more accessible, organizations must implement advanced identity verification methods, such as behavioral biometrics and cryptographic authentication, to counteract these emerging threats.

One of the most effective defenses against social engineering and identity fraud is security awareness training. Employees and individuals must be educated on how to recognize suspicious requests, verify the authenticity of communications, and avoid sharing sensitive information with unverified sources. Regular phishing simulations, scenario-based training, and real-world case studies help reinforce best practices and prepare users to identify and resist social engineering attempts. Organizations should also establish clear policies that require employees to verify identity-related requests through multiple channels before taking action.

Implementing multi-factor authentication (MFA) significantly reduces the risk of identity fraud by requiring additional verification beyond passwords. However, attackers have developed techniques to bypass MFA, such as MFA fatigue attacks, where they repeatedly send authentication requests until the victim approves one out of frustration. To counteract these attacks, organizations should enforce phishing-resistant MFA methods, such as hardware security keys and biometric authentication, that cannot be easily manipulated through social engineering.

Organizations must also enhance email and communication security to prevent social engineering attempts from reaching users. Email filtering solutions that use artificial intelligence and machine learning can identify phishing attempts based on sender reputation, language patterns, and embedded links. Implementing domain-based message authentication, reporting, and conformance (DMARC) policies helps prevent email spoofing, reducing the likelihood of attackers impersonating legitimate organizations. For phone-based attacks, call verification systems and automated fraud detection solutions can help identify and block suspicious numbers.

To detect identity fraud, organizations should monitor for anomalies in user behavior, access requests, and transaction patterns. Identity and access management (IAM) solutions that incorporate behavioral analytics can detect suspicious activity, such as logins from unusual locations, rapid privilege escalations, or deviations from normal work patterns. Fraud detection systems that analyze financial transactions and account activity can help identify identity fraud attempts in banking and e-commerce environments. Continuous monitoring and risk-based authentication ensure that potential identity compromises are identified and mitigated before attackers can cause significant damage.

By combining security awareness, strong authentication, advanced detection technologies, and continuous monitoring, organizations can significantly reduce the risks associated with social engineering and identity fraud. Attackers will continue to refine their tactics, but proactive security measures, employee vigilance, and robust identity protection strategies will help mitigate these threats and prevent unauthorized access to sensitive systems and data.

Detecting Anomalous Access Patterns

The ability to detect anomalous access patterns is critical for preventing identity-related security breaches. Cybercriminals increasingly rely on stolen credentials, social engineering, and privilege escalation to gain unauthorized access to corporate systems. Traditional security measures, such as firewalls and antivirus software, are often insufficient in detecting these threats because they focus on external attacks rather than monitoring legitimate user activity for suspicious behavior. By identifying deviations from normal access patterns, organizations can detect and respond to potential identity compromises before they lead to major security incidents.

Anomalous access patterns refer to deviations from typical user behavior, such as unusual login locations, inconsistent working hours, sudden spikes in data access, or repeated failed authentication attempts. These anomalies often indicate credential theft, insider threats, or compromised accounts. Modern security solutions use behavior-based analytics to compare real-time access activities against historical user data, helping to identify potential security risks.

One of the most common indicators of an identity compromise is login activity from unexpected locations or devices. If an employee typically logs in from a corporate office but suddenly accesses the system from an unfamiliar country or region, this could signal a compromised account. Attackers frequently use proxy servers and virtual private networks (VPNs) to obscure their locations, but security tools that analyze geolocation trends can flag suspicious access attempts and enforce additional authentication steps. For instance, if a user logs in from the United States and then attempts another login from Asia within minutes, the system can block access or require multi-factor authentication (MFA) to verify the user's identity.

Time-based anomalies are another critical indicator of unauthorized access. Most users follow consistent working hours based on their role and time zone. A sudden shift in login patterns—such as late-night or weekend access from an employee who typically works standard office hours—may indicate that an attacker has gained access to their credentials. Security monitoring solutions analyze access logs to identify irregular time-based behavior and trigger alerts for further investigation.

The volume and type of data accessed can also reveal anomalies. Employees generally interact with a specific set of files, databases, and applications relevant to their job functions. If a user suddenly downloads a large volume of sensitive data, accesses restricted areas of the network, or interacts with systems outside their usual workflow, this may indicate a security breach. Attackers who gain access to corporate environments often attempt to exfiltrate as much information as possible before detection. Implementing data loss prevention (DLP) solutions and monitoring data access patterns helps detect these threats and prevent unauthorized data exfiltration.

Privileged account activity is a key area of focus when detecting anomalous access patterns. Administrative and high-privilege accounts have greater access rights and are frequently targeted by attackers. Anomalous behavior within these accounts, such as privilege escalation, unauthorized changes to security settings, or the creation of new administrative accounts, should trigger immediate security reviews. Privileged Access Management (PAM) solutions help mitigate these risks by enforcing least privilege access, monitoring session activity, and requiring just-in-time (JIT) access approvals for high-risk actions.

Repeated failed authentication attempts often indicate brute-force attacks or credential stuffing attempts. If a system detects multiple failed logins from the same IP address or distributed login attempts across different accounts, this could suggest that an attacker is trying to guess passwords or use stolen credentials. Implementing account lockout policies, rate limiting, and adaptive authentication helps prevent unauthorized access attempts. Advanced security solutions can also use risk-based authentication, adjusting security requirements based on the likelihood of an attack. For example, if a login attempt is detected from a high-risk IP address, the system may require an additional authentication factor or block access entirely.

Session anomalies can also indicate compromised accounts. Attackers often hijack active sessions to bypass authentication controls and gain persistent access to systems. If a user's session lasts significantly longer than usual or exhibits erratic activity, such as rapidly switching between applications or accessing multiple sensitive areas, it could indicate an attacker has taken over the session. Organizations can mitigate these threats by enforcing automatic session timeouts, requiring reauthentication for high-risk actions, and monitoring session behavior in real-time.

Insider threats can also be detected through anomalous access patterns. Unlike external attackers, insiders already have legitimate access to corporate resources, making their activity harder to distinguish from normal behavior. However, significant deviations from established work patterns—such as an HR employee suddenly accessing engineering databases or a salesperson downloading financial reports—can signal potential insider threats. User and Entity Behavior Analytics (UEBA) solutions track user activity over time, creating behavioral baselines that help detect insider threats before they cause damage.

Cloud environments introduce additional challenges in detecting anomalous access patterns. Employees access cloud applications from multiple devices and locations, making it more difficult to define what constitutes "normal" behavior. Attackers often exploit cloud identity misconfigurations, weak API security, and compromised cloud credentials to gain unauthorized access. Cloud Access Security Brokers (CASBs) and Security Information and Event Management (SIEM) systems help detect suspicious cloud access by analyzing identity-related events across multiple platforms. Integrating cloud security monitoring with on-premises identity management solutions provides a comprehensive view of access patterns.

Automating the detection of anomalous access patterns reduces the burden on security teams and improves response times. Artificial intelligence (AI) and machine learning (ML) models analyze large volumes of identity-related data, identifying correlations and predicting potential threats. AI-driven security tools continuously adapt to evolving threats, refining detection models based on new attack patterns and behavioral changes. By automating identity threat detection, organizations can respond to anomalies in real time, minimizing the impact of security incidents.

Organizations should establish clear incident response protocols for handling anomalous access detections. Security teams must have predefined workflows for investigating alerts, validating threats, and taking corrective actions. Automated response mechanisms, such as temporarily disabling accounts, enforcing step-up authentication, or isolating compromised sessions, help contain threats before they escalate. Regular security training for employees ensures that users understand how to recognize and report suspicious access attempts.

By implementing robust monitoring, analytics-driven security solutions, and proactive response measures, organizations can effectively detect and mitigate anomalous access patterns. Attackers continuously evolve their tactics, but by leveraging advanced threat detection technologies and enforcing strict identity security policies, businesses can stay ahead of emerging threats and protect their sensitive data from unauthorized access.

The Role of AI and Machine Learning in Identity Security

Artificial Intelligence (AI) and Machine Learning (ML) have become essential tools in the fight against identity-based cyber threats. As organizations increasingly rely on digital identities for authentication, authorization, and access control, attackers continue to develop more sophisticated methods to bypass security measures. Traditional identity security solutions, which rely on rule-based policies and static authentication mechanisms, often struggle to detect modern identity threats. AI and ML enhance identity security by providing adaptive, data-driven approaches to threat detection, anomaly detection, and automated response mechanisms, making identity protection more dynamic and effective.

One of the key applications of AI in identity security is detecting anomalous behavior. Attackers who gain access to compromised credentials often attempt to blend in with legitimate users to avoid detection. However, even if they use valid credentials, their behavior is unlikely to perfectly match that of the legitimate user. AI-powered behavioral analytics continuously monitor login patterns, access requests, and activity logs to identify deviations from normal user behavior. For example, if an employee who typically logs in from the same location and device suddenly accesses critical systems from an unfamiliar region, an AI-driven system can flag the activity as suspicious and trigger additional authentication requirements or block access.

Machine learning models excel at detecting identity-related threats by analyzing vast amounts of data and identifying patterns that may not be apparent to human analysts. Traditional security approaches rely on predefined rules, such as blocking logins from specific locations or requiring multi-factor authentication (MFA) for high-risk activities. While these rules are effective to some extent, they often result in false positives or fail to detect new attack techniques. ML models, on the other hand, adapt and improve over time by learning from historical data, allowing them to recognize emerging threats and refine detection capabilities.

Credential theft and phishing attacks are among the most common identity-related threats, and AI is playing a critical role in mitigating these risks. AI-powered email security solutions analyze email content, sender reputation, and attachment behaviors to detect phishing attempts in real time. By using natural language processing (NLP) and deep learning, these systems can identify subtle indicators of phishing, such as impersonation attempts or urgent requests for credential resets. Unlike traditional spam filters, AI-based solutions continuously adapt to new phishing tactics, improving their detection accuracy over time.

Multi-factor authentication (MFA) is a widely used security measure, but attackers have developed methods to bypass it through social engineering and automated attacks. AI enhances MFA by introducing risk-based authentication, which dynamically adjusts security requirements based on user behavior and risk levels. Instead of enforcing MFA for every login attempt, AI-driven systems assess contextual factors such as device reputation, user history, and geolocation to determine whether additional authentication steps are necessary. If a login attempt appears high-risk, the system can enforce stricter authentication requirements, such as biometric verification or one-time passcodes, reducing the risk of account takeovers.

Insider threats pose a unique challenge in identity security because malicious insiders already have legitimate access to critical systems. AI-powered User and Entity Behavior Analytics (UEBA) help organizations detect insider threats by analyzing deviations in access behavior. For example, if an employee suddenly accesses confidential files outside of their typical job function, downloads large amounts of data, or modifies access permissions without prior authorization, AI-driven UEBA systems can flag these activities for further investigation. By continuously learning from normal user behavior, UEBA minimizes false positives while improving threat detection accuracy.

The integration of AI and ML in identity governance and administration (IGA) also improves the efficiency of access control and compliance management. Organizations often struggle with managing access permissions, especially in large enterprises with thousands of users. ML-driven IGA solutions automate the process of reviewing and adjusting access privileges based on user roles, job functions, and risk levels. By analyzing historical access patterns, AI can recommend least privilege access policies, ensuring that users only have access to the resources necessary for their roles. Additionally, AI-powered identity governance solutions help organizations comply with regulatory requirements by identifying and remediating access control violations before they lead to security incidents.

AI also plays a critical role in securing machine identities, which include service accounts, API keys, and automated scripts used in cloud environments. Attackers often target machine identities to gain access to sensitive data or manipulate cloud resources. AI-powered identity security solutions monitor machine identity usage and detect anomalies, such as unauthorized API calls or unexpected privilege escalations. By automating the detection and response to machine identity threats, organizations can prevent attackers from exploiting weakly secured service accounts.

Threat intelligence is another area where AI and ML significantly enhance identity security. AI-driven threat intelligence platforms analyze data from multiple sources, including dark web forums, breach databases, and real-time attack telemetry, to identify emerging identity threats. These platforms help organizations proactively detect credential leaks, track malicious actors, and adjust security policies based on evolving threat landscapes. By integrating AI-powered threat intelligence with identity security systems, organizations can anticipate and mitigate identity-related threats before they cause harm.

Automation and AI-driven response mechanisms are transforming how organizations handle identity security incidents. Traditional security operations teams often struggle to keep up with the volume of identity-related alerts, leading to delays in responding to threats. AI-powered security orchestration, automation, and response (SOAR) platforms streamline incident response by automatically investigating alerts, correlating identity-related data, and executing predefined remediation actions. For example, if AI detects a compromised account attempting to escalate privileges, the SOAR platform can automatically disable the account, notify security teams, and initiate a forensic investigation.

While AI and ML bring significant advantages to identity security, they are not without challenges. One of the primary concerns is adversarial AI, where attackers use AI-driven techniques to evade detection and bypass security controls. Attackers are developing sophisticated deepfake technologies to impersonate executives, automate phishing campaigns, and manipulate AI-powered authentication systems. Organizations must continuously refine AI models, implement robust anomaly detection measures, and use multi-layered security approaches to stay ahead of adversarial AI threats.

Another challenge is ensuring that AI-driven identity security solutions remain transparent and interpretable. Many AI models operate as "black boxes," making it difficult for security teams to understand why a particular activity was flagged as suspicious. Organizations must balance AI automation with human oversight, ensuring that security teams can review and validate AI-driven decisions. By combining AI's speed and scalability with human expertise, organizations can create a more effective and resilient identity security strategy.

AI and ML are revolutionizing identity security by enabling proactive threat detection, adaptive authentication, automated response mechanisms, and intelligent identity governance. As identity-based attacks continue to evolve, AI-driven security solutions provide organizations with the tools needed to detect anomalies, mitigate risks, and respond to threats in real time. By leveraging AI-powered behavioral analytics, risk-based authentication, and automated security processes, organizations can strengthen their identity security posture and protect against emerging cyber threats.

Identity Threat Hunting Techniques

Identity threat hunting is a proactive security approach that focuses on detecting and mitigating identity-based attacks before they cause significant damage. Unlike traditional security methods that rely on alerts and reactive incident response, threat hunting involves actively searching for signs of compromise within identity and access management (IAM) systems, authentication logs, and user behavior analytics. Cybercriminals frequently target identities—such as user credentials, privileged accounts, and authentication mechanisms—to gain unauthorized access, escalate privileges, and move laterally within organizations. By employing advanced identity threat hunting techniques, security teams can identify hidden threats, detect compromised accounts, and prevent identity-based breaches.

One of the most effective techniques in identity threat hunting is anomaly detection within authentication logs. Attackers who obtain stolen credentials often attempt to log in from new locations, unfamiliar devices, or unusual time zones. By analyzing authentication logs and comparing them to historical user behavior, threat hunters can identify suspicious login patterns. For example, if an employee who typically works from New York suddenly logs in from a foreign country with no prior travel history, it could indicate a compromised account. Security teams can set up threat-hunting queries that search for high-risk authentication patterns, such as multiple failed login attempts followed by a successful login from an unusual location.

Lateral movement detection is another critical aspect of identity threat hunting. Once attackers gain access to an initial account, they often attempt to escalate privileges and move across systems undetected. Threat hunters analyze authentication requests, group membership changes, and privilege escalation attempts to identify unauthorized lateral movement. One common technique used by attackers is pass-the-hash (PtH), where they steal hashed passwords and use them to authenticate without needing plaintext credentials. By monitoring for abnormal authentication token usage and privilege escalation attempts, security teams can detect lateral movement early and contain the threat before it spreads.

Monitoring service accounts and non-human identities is also an essential identity threat hunting strategy. Many organizations rely on automated scripts, application accounts, and service accounts that have persistent credentials and elevated privileges. Attackers often target these accounts because they are less frequently monitored and may have weak security controls. Threat hunters should analyze the behavior of service accounts, looking for unusual access patterns, unauthorized API calls, or modifications to IAM policies. Any deviation from the typical behavior of these accounts may indicate an attempt to exploit weakly secured machine identities.

Threat hunting also involves investigating anomalies in multi-factor authentication (MFA) usage. While MFA significantly enhances security, attackers have developed methods to bypass it using techniques such as MFA fatigue attacks, SIM swapping, and real-time phishing proxies. Security teams can analyze MFA logs to detect repeated MFA push notifications that may indicate an attacker trying to overwhelm a user into approving an unauthorized login. Additionally, sudden changes in MFA methods—such as a user switching from app-based authentication to SMS-based authentication—could indicate an attacker attempting to bypass stronger authentication mechanisms.

Behavioral analytics and User and Entity Behavior Analytics (UEBA) play a crucial role in identity threat hunting by providing insights into abnormal user activities. UEBA solutions establish a baseline of normal behavior for each user and detect deviations that could indicate a compromised account. Threat hunters use UEBA data to identify unusual file access, sudden spikes in data downloads, or unauthorized modifications to security settings. For instance, if a finance department employee suddenly accesses engineering documents or downloads large volumes of sensitive data, it could indicate an insider threat or a compromised account being used for data exfiltration.

Threat hunting also extends to identity governance and privileged access management (PAM) systems. Attackers often attempt to create new privileged accounts, modify existing permissions, or add backdoor access mechanisms to maintain persistence. Security teams should analyze changes in IAM policies, detect newly created administrator accounts, and monitor permission modifications for anomalies. Any unauthorized addition of privileged roles or sudden escalation of access rights should be investigated immediately.

Advanced threat hunting techniques involve analyzing dark web activity and threat intelligence feeds for signs of credential exposure. Attackers frequently sell or distribute stolen credentials on underground forums, which can later be used in credential stuffing or brute-force attacks. Security teams can use threat intelligence platforms to monitor for corporate email addresses, usernames, or leaked credentials appearing in breach data. If a match is found, organizations can proactively reset affected credentials, enforce stronger authentication requirements, and investigate whether the compromised credentials have been used within their environment.

Hunting for identity threats also requires monitoring for anomalous access to cloud environments. As organizations adopt cloud-based applications and identity federation services, attackers increasingly target cloud IAM configurations. Threat hunters should analyze cloud authentication logs, API access patterns, and cloud privilege escalations to detect unauthorized access. One effective technique is tracking failed login attempts from known malicious IP addresses, which may indicate an automated attack attempting to compromise cloud accounts.

Red teaming and simulated adversary tactics can also enhance identity threat hunting efforts. Security teams can conduct simulated attacks, such as phishing campaigns or simulated credential theft, to test how well their identity defenses detect and respond to threats. By replicating attacker techniques, organizations can identify weaknesses in their IAM security posture and refine their threat detection capabilities.

Automating identity threat hunting processes improves efficiency and reduces the time required to detect and respond to threats. Security orchestration, automation, and response (SOAR) platforms integrate with IAM systems, SIEM solutions, and threat intelligence feeds to automate identity threat detection and response. For example, if a compromised account is detected based on suspicious behavior, SOAR workflows can automatically disable the account, enforce a password reset, and notify security teams for further investigation.

Threat hunters should also prioritize detecting compromised insider accounts, as insiders pose a significant risk to identity security. Malicious insiders may attempt to steal sensitive data, modify access controls, or assist external attackers in bypassing security measures. By analyzing internal communications, tracking access request patterns, and monitoring privileged user activities, security teams can identify insider threats before they cause harm.

Organizations that implement robust identity threat hunting techniques can significantly improve their ability to detect, investigate, and mitigate identity-related threats. By combining anomaly detection, behavioral analytics, threat intelligence, and automation, security teams can stay ahead of attackers and protect their digital identities from compromise.

Indicators of Compromise in Identity Systems

Indicators of Compromise (IoCs) in identity systems are signs that an identity-related security breach may have occurred. Cybercriminals frequently target user accounts, authentication mechanisms, and identity management platforms to gain unauthorized access to sensitive data and critical systems. Traditional security measures often focus on detecting malware and network intrusions, but identity compromises can be more difficult to identify since attackers often use stolen credentials to blend in as legitimate users. Recognizing and responding to IoCs in identity systems is crucial for preventing unauthorized access, data breaches, and privilege escalation.

One of the most common IoCs in identity systems is unusual login activity. Attackers who gain access to stolen credentials typically attempt to log in from locations, devices, or IP addresses that do not match the legitimate user's historical patterns. If a user who normally logs in from the United States suddenly authenticates from an IP address in Eastern Europe or Asia, this could indicate a compromised account. Similarly, multiple failed login attempts followed by a successful authentication from a new location suggest that an attacker may have brute-forced a password or successfully used a stolen credential.

Mismatched device fingerprints and browser characteristics are another key IoC. Identity security systems track login sessions based on device type, browser version, operating system, and other characteristics. If a user who typically logs in from a corporate-issued laptop suddenly authenticates from an unknown mobile device or a different operating system, this could indicate an account takeover. Attackers often use virtual private networks (VPNs) or Tor networks to mask their actual location, but they cannot easily replicate the exact device characteristics of a legitimate user. Monitoring for unusual device profiles can help detect compromised accounts.

Unusual spikes in authentication failures can also indicate an identity attack. Credential stuffing, brute-force attacks, and password spraying techniques generate large volumes of failed login attempts as attackers try to guess passwords. If a particular account experiences a sudden surge in failed authentication attempts, especially from multiple IP addresses, this suggests an automated attack in progress. Security teams should investigate such activity and consider implementing rate-limiting controls, multi-factor authentication (MFA), and account lockout policies to prevent unauthorized access.

Unexpected changes to multi-factor authentication (MFA) settings can also be a strong IoC. Attackers who compromise an account will often attempt to disable or modify MFA settings to prevent legitimate users from regaining control. If a user's MFA method is changed from a more secure authentication method, such as a hardware security key, to a less secure method, such as SMS-based authentication, this could indicate an attacker is preparing to take over the account. Additionally, repeated MFA reset requests or unauthorized attempts to enroll new authentication devices should be investigated as potential compromise attempts.

Privileged account misuse is another major IoC in identity systems. Administrative and high-privilege accounts are primary targets for attackers because they provide greater access to sensitive systems and data. If a privileged user suddenly accesses resources they have never interacted with before, modifies security configurations, or creates new administrative accounts without approval, this could indicate an insider threat or an external attacker using a compromised privileged account. Security teams should continuously monitor privileged account activity, enforce least privilege access, and implement privileged access management (PAM) solutions to reduce the risk of misuse.

Anomalous access to sensitive data or applications can also signal an identity compromise. Users typically access a specific set of applications, files, and databases related to their job functions. If an employee who normally interacts with HR records suddenly starts accessing financial databases or customer payment information, this behavior should be flagged for review. Attackers who gain access to an identity will often attempt to exfiltrate large volumes of data before being detected. Security solutions should monitor data access patterns and trigger alerts when users interact with unusually large amounts of sensitive information.

Unexpected password changes or recovery requests are another red flag in identity systems. Attackers who gain access to an account often attempt to reset passwords to lock out the legitimate user. If multiple password reset requests are initiated within a short timeframe or if a user reports being unexpectedly logged out of all sessions, this may indicate an attacker is attempting to hijack the account. Organizations should enforce strong password recovery policies, require MFA for password changes, and monitor for unusual password reset requests.

Session hijacking and unusual session durations are additional IoCs. Attackers may use stolen session tokens to bypass authentication and gain persistent access to an account. If a user session lasts significantly longer than usual or exhibits erratic activity, this could indicate a hijacked session. Security teams should enforce session timeouts, require reauthentication for high-risk activities, and monitor session behaviors for anomalies.

Unauthorized API access is another identity compromise indicator, particularly in cloud environments. Many modern identity systems rely on APIs for authentication and user management. Attackers often attempt to exploit weak API security by using stolen API keys, abusing service accounts, or making unauthorized API requests. If an API key is used from an unusual location or an API account suddenly starts making high-volume requests, this could indicate an identity-related attack. Organizations should enforce strict API access controls, monitor API activity logs, and rotate API keys regularly to mitigate this risk.

Another key indicator of identity compromise is the presence of newly created or modified identity federation rules. Many organizations use identity federation and single sign-on (SSO) to simplify authentication across multiple systems. Attackers who gain access to an identity provider may attempt to modify federation rules to grant themselves persistent access or create new trust relationships with malicious identity providers. Security teams should regularly audit identity federation configurations, monitor for unauthorized changes, and enforce strong access controls on identity management platforms.

Abnormal authentication token usage is another important IoC. Attackers who gain access to OAuth tokens, SAML assertions, or other authentication tokens may use them to bypass authentication mechanisms. If a user account starts issuing an unusually high number of authentication tokens, accessing multiple systems simultaneously, or reusing old authentication tokens beyond their expiration, this could indicate a security breach. Implementing token expiration policies, using short-lived tokens, and continuously monitoring token usage can help detect and mitigate token-based identity attacks.

Detecting and responding to IoCs in identity systems requires a combination of real-time monitoring, anomaly detection, and automated response mechanisms. Security teams should implement Identity Threat Detection and Response (ITDR) solutions that integrate with identity and access management (IAM) platforms, security information and event management (SIEM) systems, and user behavior analytics (UBA) tools. By proactively hunting for identity-related IoCs, organizations can reduce the risk of account takeovers, insider threats, and unauthorized data access.

Regular identity security audits, continuous access monitoring, and user awareness training further strengthen an organization's ability to detect and prevent identity compromises. By staying vigilant for IoCs and implementing advanced identity security measures, businesses can enhance their defenses against evolving identity threats.

Incident Response for Identity Breaches

Identity breaches represent one of the most critical threats organizations face today. When attackers gain unauthorized access to user accounts, privileged credentials, or identity management systems, they can escalate privileges, exfiltrate data, and disrupt business operations. An effective incident response strategy for identity breaches is essential for minimizing damage, containing the threat, and preventing future compromises. Unlike traditional security incidents that focus on malware or network intrusions, identity breaches require a specialized approach that addresses compromised credentials, authentication mechanisms, and access controls.

The first step in responding to an identity breach is detection. Organizations must have continuous monitoring and anomaly detection in place to identify suspicious activity in identity systems. Indicators of compromise (IoCs) such as failed login attempts, unexpected multi-factor authentication (MFA) resets, unusual geographic access patterns, and unauthorized privilege escalations should trigger immediate investigation. Security Information and Event Management (SIEM) solutions, Identity Threat Detection and Response (ITDR) tools, and User and Entity Behavior Analytics (UEBA) play a crucial role in detecting identity-related threats in real time.

Once an identity breach is detected, the next priority is containment. The compromised account or identity must be isolated to prevent further unauthorized access. This may involve temporarily disabling the affected account, revoking active session tokens, and requiring immediate password resets. If a privileged account is compromised, it should be deactivated immediately, and any changes made by the attacker should be reviewed and reversed. Organizations that use Privileged Access Management (PAM) solutions can leverage just-in-time (JIT) access controls to minimize the risk of privilege escalation during an incident.

Incident response teams must also assess the scope and impact of the breach. This involves identifying which accounts, systems, and data have been affected. Security analysts should examine authentication logs, API activity, and access permissions to determine how the attacker gained access and what actions they performed. If the breach originated from a phishing attack, credential stuffing attempt, or social engineering tactic, security teams should investigate whether other users have been targeted as well.

During an identity breach investigation, organizations must also check for persistence mechanisms left by the attacker. Adversaries often create new accounts, modify access policies, or install backdoor authentication methods to maintain long-term access. Security teams should audit IAM configurations, look for unauthorized identity federation changes, and review recent administrative actions. If attackers have modified identity federation rules, they may have established persistent access to cloud applications or external services. Any suspicious identity-related modifications should be reverted, and additional authentication safeguards should be enforced.

Remediation efforts should focus on strengthening authentication mechanisms and access controls. Organizations should enforce immediate password resets for compromised accounts and implement strong MFA to prevent further unauthorized logins. If attackers bypassed MFA using SIM swapping, MFA fatigue attacks, or phishing techniques, security teams should transition to more secure authentication methods, such as FIDO2 security keys or certificate-based authentication. Additionally, enforcing least privilege access policies and conducting an organization-wide access review can help minimize exposure to future identity threats.

Communication is a vital aspect of incident response for identity breaches. Security teams must coordinate with IT, legal, compliance, and executive leadership to ensure a structured response. If the breach affects customer identities, the organization must determine its legal obligations regarding data breach notifications. Regulations such as GDPR, CCPA, and HIPAA require organizations to notify affected users, regulatory bodies, and other stakeholders when personal identity information is compromised. The response plan should include guidelines on when and how to inform users, including recommendations for securing their accounts, resetting passwords, and monitoring for further suspicious activity.

Another critical component of identity breach response is forensic analysis. Security teams must conduct a detailed investigation to determine the root cause of the incident, identify vulnerabilities in authentication systems, and assess whether any compromised accounts have been used for further malicious activities. Digital forensics tools can help analyze authentication logs, track attacker movements, and uncover any unauthorized changes made to identity management platforms. If the breach originated from third-party integrations or cloud services, forensic investigators should collaborate with external service providers to assess the extent of the compromise.

Once the immediate threat is neutralized, organizations should conduct a post-incident review to strengthen their identity security posture. This includes evaluating the effectiveness of detection mechanisms, analyzing how attackers bypassed existing security controls, and identifying areas for improvement. Security teams should update IAM policies, enhance anomaly detection rules, and implement additional identity security measures such as continuous authentication, adaptive access controls, and AI-driven identity monitoring.

Implementing automated incident response workflows can significantly reduce the time required to contain identity breaches. Security Orchestration, Automation, and Response (SOAR) platforms can integrate with IAM systems, SIEM solutions, and ITDR tools to automate threat detection, account disabling, password resets, and access revocations. By automating identity breach response, organizations can mitigate risks faster and reduce the impact of credential-based attacks.

Security awareness training is also an essential part of identity breach prevention and response. Employees must be educated on recognizing phishing attempts, avoiding password reuse, and following secure authentication practices. Organizations should conduct regular security training sessions, simulate social engineering attacks, and reinforce best practices for protecting corporate identities.

Organizations should also collaborate with external threat intelligence providers and industry groups to stay informed about emerging identity threats. Many cybercriminals sell stolen credentials on dark web marketplaces, and proactive monitoring can help organizations identify compromised accounts before they are used in attacks. Threat intelligence feeds that track credential leaks, phishing campaigns, and authentication attacks can provide valuable insights for strengthening identity security strategies.

Testing and improving incident response plans through tabletop exercises and simulated identity breaches can help organizations refine their processes. Conducting regular red team assessments and penetration tests can expose weaknesses in identity security controls, allowing security teams to address gaps before attackers can exploit them. Incident response teams should update playbooks and response procedures based on lessons learned from past incidents to ensure a more effective defense against future identity breaches.

Ultimately, an effective incident response strategy for identity breaches must combine proactive threat detection, rapid containment, thorough forensic investigation, and long-term security improvements. Organizations that continuously refine their identity security posture, automate response mechanisms, and educate their workforce on identity protection will be better equipped to defend against evolving identity threats and mitigate the impact of future breaches.

Forensic Analysis of Identity-Based Attacks

Forensic analysis of identity-based attacks is a crucial process that enables organizations to investigate security incidents, uncover attacker tactics, and implement effective remediation measures. Unlike traditional malware or network-based attacks, identity compromises often involve stolen credentials, privilege escalation, and unauthorized access attempts that mimic legitimate user behavior. This makes forensic analysis of identity-related breaches particularly challenging, requiring a combination of log analysis, behavioral analytics, and forensic techniques to identify the root cause of an attack and prevent future occurrences.

The first step in forensic analysis is preserving digital evidence. When an identity-based attack is suspected, security teams must ensure that authentication logs, access control data, session records, and system event logs are securely stored for investigation. Since attackers may attempt to erase or modify logs to cover their tracks, organizations should implement tamper-proof logging mechanisms and centralized log storage solutions. Security Information and Event Management (SIEM) platforms play a crucial role in forensic investigations by aggregating and correlating identity-related events across an organization's IT environment.

Authentication logs are one of the primary data sources for forensic analysis. Investigators examine login attempts, failed authentication events, geographic access locations, and multi-factor authentication (MFA) interactions to determine whether an identity has been compromised. A sudden change in login behavior—such as an employee accessing corporate resources from an unfamiliar country or an unusual IP address—may indicate an account takeover. Forensic analysts must trace authentication patterns over time to distinguish between legitimate travel activity and potential compromise.

Privileged access logs provide additional insight into identity-based attacks, as attackers often target high-privilege accounts to gain control over critical systems. Investigators should analyze administrative access requests, privilege escalation attempts, and modifications to IAM (Identity and Access Management) policies. If an attacker has created new administrative accounts, changed security settings, or granted excessive permissions to a compromised identity, these actions must be identified and reversed. Privileged Access Management (PAM) solutions provide valuable forensic data by recording privileged session activities and flagging unauthorized actions.

Multi-factor authentication (MFA) logs are another key component of forensic analysis. While MFA provides an additional layer of security, attackers have developed techniques to bypass MFA using SIM swapping, social engineering, or MFA fatigue attacks. Investigators should review MFA logs for abnormal behavior, such as multiple failed push notification approvals, sudden changes in authentication methods, or new device enrollments that do not match the user's historical behavior. If an attacker has successfully bypassed MFA, security teams must determine how the compromise occurred and implement stronger authentication controls, such as hardware security keys or adaptive authentication.

Session hijacking is another identity-based attack technique that requires detailed forensic investigation. Attackers who gain access to authentication tokens or session cookies can impersonate legitimate users without needing their passwords. Forensic analysts must examine session records for unusually long durations, simultaneous access from multiple locations, and suspicious session token reuse. Organizations should implement short-lived session tokens, enforce reauthentication for high-risk actions, and monitor session activity for anomalies that could indicate session hijacking attempts.

Forensic analysts also examine identity federation logs to investigate attacks that exploit Single Sign-On (SSO) and cloud identity integrations. Many organizations use identity federation to streamline authentication across cloud services, but misconfigurations or compromised identity providers can expose systems to security risks. Attackers who manipulate federation trust relationships may gain unauthorized access to multiple applications using a single compromised identity. Investigators should review identity federation logs for suspicious modifications, unauthorized identity provider changes, and unexpected cross-platform access attempts.

API and machine identity forensic analysis is another critical aspect of investigating identity-based attacks. Many organizations rely on API keys, service accounts, and machine identities for automated workflows and cloud service integrations. Attackers often exploit weak API security by stealing authentication tokens or abusing overly permissive service accounts. Investigators should analyze API logs for anomalous requests, unauthorized API calls, and privilege escalations. Organizations should implement least-privilege access policies for machine identities, rotate API keys regularly, and monitor API activity for signs of credential abuse.

Dark web monitoring can provide valuable intelligence in forensic investigations by identifying whether compromised credentials have been leaked or sold on underground forums. Attackers frequently distribute stolen usernames, passwords, and authentication tokens for use in credential stuffing attacks. By leveraging threat intelligence feeds and dark web monitoring services, forensic analysts can determine whether an identity compromise originated from a prior data breach or phishing campaign. If compromised credentials are discovered, organizations should enforce mandatory password resets, implement account monitoring, and notify affected users of potential risks.

Digital forensics tools such as endpoint detection and response (EDR) solutions can help trace identity compromises back to their source. If an attacker has gained initial access through a phishing attack, forensic analysts should examine email headers, attachments, and web traffic logs to identify the phishing vector. Similarly, if malware such as keyloggers or credential-stealing Trojans were used to capture authentication credentials, forensic teams must analyze infected endpoints to remove malicious software and prevent further compromise.

One of the most challenging aspects of forensic analysis is differentiating between insider threats and external attackers. Malicious insiders may abuse their legitimate access to exfiltrate data, modify access controls, or escalate privileges for unauthorized actions. Behavioral analytics can help identify insider threats by analyzing deviations from normal user behavior. If an employee suddenly accesses sensitive data outside of business hours, downloads large volumes of files, or attempts to disable security controls, these actions may indicate an insider threat requiring further investigation.

Forensic analysis should also include a post-attack review to assess security gaps and implement stronger defenses. Once investigators have determined the root cause of an identity-based attack, organizations must update their identity security policies, enforce stricter access controls, and implement automated detection mechanisms to prevent similar incidents in the future. Security teams should conduct red team exercises and penetration testing to simulate identity compromise scenarios and evaluate their response capabilities.

Organizations that establish a comprehensive forensic analysis framework for identity-based attacks will be better equipped to detect, investigate, and mitigate security incidents. By leveraging authentication logs, privileged access monitoring, MFA analytics, and machine identity security, forensic investigators can uncover attacker tactics, strengthen identity security defenses, and minimize the impact of identity compromises.

SIEM and Identity Threat Correlation

Security Information and Event Management (SIEM) solutions play a crucial role in detecting and responding to identity threats by aggregating and analyzing security events across an organization's IT environment. As identity-based attacks become more sophisticated, organizations must move beyond static rule-based detection and leverage SIEM platforms to correlate identity-related data from multiple sources. By integrating authentication logs, access control events, privileged account activity, and behavioral analytics, SIEM solutions enable security teams to identify anomalous patterns that indicate identity compromise.

One of the primary functions of SIEM in identity security is collecting and centralizing identity-related logs from various sources, including Identity and Access Management (IAM) systems, directory services, cloud authentication platforms, and multi-factor authentication (MFA) providers. These logs contain valuable information about user login attempts, failed authentications, privilege escalations, and unusual access requests. By continuously analyzing this data, SIEM platforms help security teams detect identity-based attacks, such as account takeovers, credential stuffing, and insider threats.

Identity threat correlation in SIEM involves linking multiple security events to identify patterns that may indicate an attack in progress. Attackers often try to evade detection by spreading their activities across different systems and using compromised credentials to blend in with legitimate users. SIEM solutions use correlation rules, machine learning, and behavioral analytics to piece together related events and provide a comprehensive view of identity threats. For example, a failed login attempt followed by a successful authentication from an unusual location and an administrative privilege escalation within a short time window could indicate a compromised account.

SIEM platforms also help detect anomalous login behaviors by analyzing authentication patterns across multiple environments. If a user who normally logs in from the corporate office suddenly accesses cloud services from an unfamiliar geographic region, the SIEM system can trigger an alert. Correlating this event with other identity-related data, such as new MFA enrollments or changes in device fingerprints, can help security teams determine whether the login is legitimate or part of an identity attack. By continuously refining correlation rules based on historical data and evolving attack techniques, SIEM solutions improve the accuracy of identity threat detection.

Another critical aspect of SIEM-based identity threat correlation is monitoring privileged account activity. Privileged users, such as system administrators, database managers, and cloud service operators, have elevated access rights that make them attractive targets for attackers. SIEM solutions track privileged account usage, detecting unauthorized access attempts, unusual privilege escalations, and administrative actions that deviate from normal behavior. If a privileged account starts accessing resources outside its usual scope or executes commands inconsistent with its role, SIEM can flag the activity for investigation.

SIEM integration with User and Entity Behavior Analytics (UEBA) enhances identity threat correlation by applying machine learning algorithms to detect behavioral anomalies. Unlike static correlation rules, UEBA adapts to evolving identity threats by continuously analyzing user behavior patterns. If an employee who typically accesses a specific set of applications suddenly begins interacting with high-risk systems, the SIEM platform can trigger a risk-based alert. By combining SIEM and UEBA, organizations gain deeper visibility into identity-related threats and reduce false positives associated with traditional security alerts.

Multi-factor authentication (MFA) log analysis is another important component of identity threat detection in SIEM. Attackers often attempt to bypass MFA through techniques such as SIM swapping, MFA fatigue attacks, and phishing proxies. SIEM solutions monitor

MFA logs for signs of compromise, such as multiple failed MFA attempts, new device enrollments from suspicious locations, or users suddenly switching to weaker authentication methods. If a user repeatedly declines push authentication requests before approving one, it could indicate an attacker trying to overwhelm the victim into granting access. SIEM can correlate these MFA anomalies with other identity-related events to determine if an account takeover is occurring.

Cloud identity security presents additional challenges that SIEM solutions help address. Many organizations use cloud-based IAM solutions, such as Azure Active Directory, Okta, or Google Workspace, which generate authentication and access logs separate from on-premises systems. SIEM platforms integrate cloud identity data, allowing security teams to detect cross-environment threats. If a user logs into a corporate VPN using an on-premises Active Directory account and simultaneously accesses cloud services from an unrecognized device, SIEM can correlate these events to identify potential credential compromise.

Threat intelligence integration further enhances SIEM's ability to detect identity threats. Many SIEM platforms incorporate threat intelligence feeds that provide real-time data on compromised credentials, known malicious IP addresses, and adversary tactics. By correlating identity events with threat intelligence, SIEM can detect login attempts from blacklisted IP addresses, identify users whose credentials have appeared in dark web data breaches, and block authentication requests from high-risk locations. Proactively monitoring identity-related threat intelligence helps organizations prevent account takeovers before they occur.

Incident response automation is another key benefit of SIEM-based identity threat correlation. When SIEM detects an identity-related threat, it can trigger automated response actions, such as temporarily disabling compromised accounts, forcing password resets, or requiring step-up authentication. Security Orchestration, Automation, and Response (SOAR) platforms extend SIEM capabilities by integrating with IAM systems to enforce real-time security policies. For example, if SIEM detects that a privileged account has been compromised, SOAR can automatically revoke its access and initiate an investigation. By automating incident response workflows, organizations reduce the time required to mitigate identity breaches.

SIEM platforms also support compliance monitoring and audit reporting for identity security. Many regulatory frameworks, such as GDPR, HIPAA, and SOX, require organizations to maintain detailed logs of identity-related activities. SIEM solutions provide centralized logging, real-time compliance checks, and automated reporting, ensuring that organizations can demonstrate adherence to security policies. By correlating identity events across multiple environments, SIEM enables auditors to trace access control changes, detect policy violations, and ensure compliance with identity security standards.

As identity threats continue to evolve, organizations must adopt an adaptive security approach that leverages SIEM and identity threat correlation. By integrating authentication logs, behavioral analytics, privileged access monitoring, and threat intelligence, SIEM solutions provide a holistic view of identity security risks. Security teams can proactively detect identity-based attacks, automate response actions, and continuously refine detection strategies to stay ahead of emerging threats. By effectively using SIEM for identity security, organizations strengthen their defenses against credential compromises, insider threats, and unauthorized access attempts.

Identity Threats in Supply Chain Attacks

Supply chain attacks have become a significant cybersecurity concern, as attackers increasingly target vendors, third-party service providers, and software supply chains to infiltrate organizations. These attacks exploit trust relationships between businesses and their suppliers, leveraging compromised identities to gain unauthorized access to critical systems. Identity threats in supply chain attacks pose a unique challenge because they exploit the interconnected nature of modern enterprises, making it difficult to detect and mitigate unauthorized access before substantial damage occurs.

One of the primary ways attackers compromise identities in supply chain attacks is by targeting third-party credentials. Many organizations rely on vendors, contractors, and cloud service providers that require access to corporate systems. If an attacker compromises a vendor's credentials—whether through phishing, credential stuffing, or malware—they can use those credentials to impersonate legitimate users and move laterally within the target organization's network. Because these third-party accounts often have elevated privileges, attackers can bypass traditional security controls and access sensitive data.

Identity federation and single sign-on (SSO) systems introduce additional risks in supply chain attacks. Many organizations use federated identity management to allow seamless authentication across multiple platforms, including third-party services. If an attacker gains access to a compromised identity within the supply chain, they may be able to exploit trust relationships between identity providers and target organizations. By abusing SSO mechanisms, attackers can move between different applications and cloud environments without triggering security alerts, making detection more challenging.

Another major risk in supply chain attacks comes from compromised software development and code-signing credentials. Attackers who gain access to a software vendor's identity system can inject malicious code into legitimate software updates. This tactic was demonstrated in high-profile attacks such as the SolarWinds breach, where attackers inserted backdoors into widely used IT management software. Organizations that relied on the compromised software unknowingly allowed attackers to infiltrate their networks. Because these attacks leverage legitimate digital signatures and authentication mechanisms, they often evade traditional security defenses.

Insider threats within the supply chain also pose a significant risk. Employees of third-party vendors or contractors may have legitimate access to critical systems, making them potential targets for attackers. Malicious insiders can abuse their access to exfiltrate sensitive data, modify configurations, or facilitate unauthorized access for external threat actors. Additionally, negligent insiders who fall victim to phishing attacks or fail to follow security best practices can inadvertently expose supply chain credentials to attackers.

Attackers also exploit weak authentication and access control policies within the supply chain. Many vendors and third-party partners use shared accounts, default passwords, or outdated authentication methods that provide an easy entry point for attackers. Organizations that do not enforce strong multi-factor authentication (MFA) or least-privilege access policies risk allowing compromised identities to be used for unauthorized activities. Once an attacker gains a foothold through weak authentication mechanisms, they can escalate privileges and gain deeper access to the target organization's systems.

Privileged access abuse is another critical identity threat in supply chain attacks. Many vendors and service providers require administrative access to corporate systems to perform maintenance, troubleshooting, or software deployments. If an attacker compromises a privileged vendor account, they can manipulate security settings, disable monitoring tools, and create backdoor accounts for persistent access. Organizations must implement strict Privileged Access Management (PAM) controls to limit the exposure of privileged supply chain accounts and monitor their activities in real time.

Cloud environments introduce additional identity threats in supply chain attacks. Many organizations rely on cloud-based Software-as-a-Service (SaaS) applications, Infrastructure-as-a-Service (IaaS) platforms, and third-party integrations that require API keys, OAuth tokens, and service accounts. If attackers compromise these credentials, they can manipulate cloud resources, exfiltrate data, and launch further attacks from within the victim's cloud environment. Cloud Identity and Access Management (Cloud IAM) solutions must enforce strong authentication policies, regularly rotate API keys, and monitor cloud identity activity to prevent unauthorized access.

One of the most effective ways to mitigate identity threats in supply chain attacks is by implementing Zero Trust security principles. A Zero Trust approach assumes that no identity—whether internal or external—should be trusted by default. Instead, organizations must continuously verify the identity, device, and behavior of every user attempting to access critical systems. By enforcing continuous authentication, risk-based access controls, and micro-segmentation, organizations can reduce the likelihood of supply chain identity compromises leading to full-scale breaches.

Identity threat detection and response (ITDR) solutions play a crucial role in identifying supply chain attacks before they escalate. These solutions analyze identity-related events, such as unusual login activity, privilege escalation attempts, and anomalous API access, to detect potential supply chain threats. By correlating identity data from multiple sources, ITDR platforms can flag suspicious behavior that may indicate an ongoing supply chain attack. Automated response mechanisms can then disable compromised accounts, revoke access permissions, and trigger incident response workflows.

Organizations must also conduct regular identity risk assessments for their supply chain partners. Vendor security assessments should evaluate the authentication methods, identity governance policies, and access controls used by third-party providers. Organizations should enforce strict identity security requirements in vendor contracts, including mandatory MFA enforcement, least-privilege access controls, and regular access reviews. Supply chain partners that fail to meet these security standards should be required to implement additional safeguards before being granted access to critical systems.

Monitoring identity-related threat intelligence is another important defense strategy. Cybercriminals frequently sell stolen supply chain credentials on dark web marketplaces or use them in targeted attacks against high-value organizations. Threat intelligence platforms that track credential leaks, phishing campaigns, and identity fraud can help organizations identify compromised supply chain accounts before they are exploited. Security teams should use this intelligence to proactively reset compromised credentials, notify affected vendors, and implement additional security measures.

Incident response planning is essential for mitigating the impact of identity threats in supply chain attacks. Organizations must have predefined response procedures for detecting, containing, and remediating identity compromises related to third-party vendors. Incident response teams should conduct tabletop exercises that simulate supply chain identity breaches to ensure they can respond effectively in real-world scenarios. Additionally, security teams should establish clear communication channels with supply chain partners to coordinate rapid threat mitigation efforts when an identity compromise is detected.

To strengthen identity security in the supply chain, organizations should invest in advanced authentication technologies such as passwordless authentication, behavioral biometrics, and continuous authentication. Passwordless authentication methods, such as FIDO2 security keys and certificate-based authentication, reduce the reliance on traditional passwords, making it harder for attackers to steal credentials. Behavioral biometrics analyze user actions, such as typing speed and mouse movements, to detect anomalous behavior and prevent unauthorized access. Continuous authentication ensures that identity verification is not a one-time event but an ongoing process that adapts to real-time risk factors.

By implementing strong identity security measures, enforcing strict vendor access controls, and leveraging advanced threat detection technologies, organizations can reduce the risk of identity threats in supply chain attacks. As attackers continue to exploit third-party relationships to infiltrate organizations, businesses must remain proactive in securing supply chain identities and preventing unauthorized access to critical systems.

The Impact of Ransomware on Identity Security

Ransomware attacks have evolved into one of the most devastating cybersecurity threats, targeting businesses, government agencies, and critical infrastructure worldwide. While ransomware is traditionally associated with data encryption and financial extortion, its impact on identity security is equally severe. Attackers often exploit weak identity and access management (IAM) policies, compromised credentials, and privileged accounts to deploy ransomware, escalate their access, and maximize damage. As ransomware tactics continue to evolve, organizations must strengthen identity security to prevent unauthorized access and minimize the impact of these attacks.

One of the primary ways ransomware actors gain access to an organization's network is through compromised identities. Cybercriminals frequently use phishing attacks, credential stuffing, and brute-force techniques to obtain user credentials. Once inside, attackers impersonate legitimate users to bypass security controls and move laterally within the network. Unlike traditional malware infections, which rely on software vulnerabilities, identity-based ransomware attacks exploit weak authentication mechanisms and poor identity hygiene to gain persistence and escalate privileges.

Multi-factor authentication (MFA) is one of the most effective defenses against identity-based ransomware attacks, yet many organizations fail to enforce it consistently. Attackers who obtain stolen credentials can easily access systems that lack MFA protection. Even when MFA is in place, attackers have developed techniques such as MFA fatigue attacks, real-time phishing proxies, and SIM swapping to bypass these defenses. Security teams must implement phishing-resistant MFA methods, such as hardware security keys or biometric authentication, to reduce the risk of unauthorized access.

Once ransomware operators gain access to a network, they often seek out privileged accounts to maximize their impact. Privileged Access Management (PAM) solutions help mitigate this risk by enforcing least privilege access, requiring just-in-time (JIT) privilege elevation, and monitoring privileged account activity. Without PAM controls, attackers can use compromised administrator credentials to disable security tools, delete backups, and spread ransomware across multiple systems. Organizations that fail to protect privileged accounts face a significantly higher risk of widespread ransomware infection.

Lateral movement is a key strategy in ransomware campaigns, allowing attackers to spread from the initial point of compromise to critical systems. Identity security plays a crucial role in preventing lateral movement by enforcing strict access controls, monitoring for anomalous authentication patterns, and implementing network segmentation. Attackers often exploit misconfigured Single Sign-On (SSO) systems, weak identity federation settings, and excessive access permissions to move undetected between on-premises and cloud environments. Security teams must continuously audit IAM policies to identify and remediate overly permissive access rights.

Ransomware operators increasingly target Active Directory (AD) as a primary attack vector. AD is a central component of enterprise identity management, controlling authentication and authorization across the network. Attackers who compromise AD can create new accounts, reset passwords, and escalate privileges to deploy ransomware at scale. AD misconfigurations, such as weak Kerberos ticket policies, unprotected domain controllers, and excessive administrative privileges, provide attackers with opportunities to escalate their attacks. Organizations should implement AD security best practices, such as enabling tiered administrative access, enforcing secure authentication protocols, and continuously monitoring AD activity for suspicious changes.

Cloud identity security is also at risk in ransomware attacks, as many organizations store sensitive data and applications in cloud environments. Attackers who gain access to cloud IAM systems can exfiltrate data, encrypt cloud workloads, and disrupt operations. Cloud-based ransomware attacks often exploit misconfigured identity permissions, weak API security, and compromised service accounts. Security teams must enforce least privilege access in cloud IAM policies, monitor cloud authentication logs, and implement conditional access controls to prevent unauthorized cloud access.

Data exfiltration has become a common tactic in modern ransomware attacks, where attackers steal sensitive information before encrypting systems. Identity security plays a critical role in detecting and preventing data theft by monitoring for abnormal data access patterns. If a user account suddenly downloads large volumes of data, accesses restricted files, or attempts to disable security monitoring, it may indicate an impending ransomware attack. Security teams should implement real-time identity analytics, enforce data loss prevention (DLP) policies, and use behavioral analytics to detect suspicious identity activities before data is compromised.

Incident response planning for ransomware attacks must include identity security considerations. Organizations should have predefined protocols for detecting, containing, and remediating identity compromises associated with ransomware infections. Automated response mechanisms, such as disabling compromised accounts, revoking access tokens, and enforcing step-up authentication, can help limit the impact of an attack. Security teams should also conduct regular ransomware simulation exercises to test their identity breach response capabilities and identify areas for improvement.

Post-attack identity recovery is another critical aspect of ransomware response. Once an organization regains control of its systems, all compromised identities must be audited and secured. Security teams should reset all affected passwords, rotate authentication tokens, and conduct a thorough review of IAM policies to ensure that attackers have not established persistent access. In cases where privileged accounts were compromised, organizations should implement additional PAM controls, such as requiring manual approval for privilege elevation and enforcing continuous session monitoring.

Threat intelligence plays an essential role in defending against identity-based ransomware attacks. Security teams should monitor for leaked credentials, track ransomware operator tactics, and stay informed about emerging attack techniques. Many ransomware groups share stolen credentials on underground forums or sell them on dark web marketplaces before launching an attack. By integrating threat intelligence feeds with IAM systems, organizations can proactively identify and mitigate identity threats before they escalate into full-scale ransomware incidents.

Identity hygiene is a fundamental component of ransomware defense. Organizations must enforce strong password policies, eliminate unnecessary accounts, and regularly audit access permissions. Attackers frequently exploit dormant accounts, weak passwords, and outdated authentication mechanisms to infiltrate networks. Security teams should implement identity lifecycle management processes that automatically deprovision inactive accounts, enforce password rotation policies, and require MFA for all administrative actions.

The financial and operational impact of ransomware extends beyond encrypted systems, affecting business continuity, reputation, and regulatory compliance. Identity-related breaches resulting from ransomware attacks can lead to legal penalties, data privacy violations, and loss of customer trust. Organizations that fail to secure their identity infrastructure may face prolonged recovery times and higher ransom demands. Implementing a comprehensive identity security strategy reduces the likelihood of ransomware success and strengthens overall cyber resilience.

By integrating identity security best practices with ransomware defense strategies, organizations can mitigate the risk of identity compromise, limit lateral movement, and detect ransomware activity before it causes irreversible damage. Continuous monitoring, adaptive authentication, and strong access controls are essential for preventing identity-based ransomware attacks and ensuring that identities remain secure in the face of evolving threats.

Phishing and Identity Exploitation

Phishing remains one of the most effective and widely used attack vectors for compromising identities. Cybercriminals use phishing to deceive users into revealing sensitive credentials, multi-factor authentication (MFA) tokens, or personal information that can be leveraged for identity exploitation. Unlike traditional hacking techniques that exploit software vulnerabilities, phishing attacks target human psychology, relying on social engineering to trick victims into providing access to their accounts. As organizations increasingly adopt identity-centric security models, attackers have evolved their phishing tactics to bypass modern authentication mechanisms, making identity security a critical defense against these threats.

One of the most common forms of phishing is email-based credential harvesting, where attackers send fraudulent emails impersonating trusted entities such as corporate IT departments, financial institutions, or cloud service providers. These emails often contain urgent messages instructing recipients to reset their passwords, verify their accounts, or approve transactions. When victims click on the embedded links, they are redirected to fake login pages designed to mimic legitimate authentication portals. Unsuspecting users enter their credentials, unknowingly providing attackers with direct access to their accounts. Once stolen, these credentials can be used to compromise corporate systems, perform identity fraud, or escalate privileges.

Spear-phishing attacks take this technique further by targeting specific individuals within an organization. Attackers research their victims using publicly available information, such as LinkedIn profiles, company websites, and social media accounts, to craft highly personalized phishing messages. For example, an attacker may impersonate a company executive, sending an email to a finance team member requesting an urgent wire transfer. Because the email appears to come from a trusted source and contains personalized details, the recipient is more likely to comply without verifying its authenticity. Spear-phishing is particularly dangerous because it is difficult to detect using traditional spam filters and security tools.

Business Email Compromise (BEC) is another advanced form of phishing that exploits identity trust relationships. Attackers gain access to corporate email accounts, often through credential theft, and use them to send fraudulent messages to employees, partners, or customers. In many cases, attackers insert themselves into ongoing email conversations, subtly modifying details such as payment instructions, invoice numbers, or bank account details to divert funds. Because these messages originate from legitimate accounts, victims often fail to recognize the deception until financial losses have occurred. Organizations must implement robust email security controls, such as domain-based message authentication (DMARC) policies and anomaly detection, to mitigate the risks of BEC.

Vishing (voice phishing) and smishing (SMS phishing) extend phishing attacks beyond email by leveraging phone calls and text messages to trick victims into revealing sensitive information. In vishing attacks, cybercriminals pose as customer service representatives, IT support personnel, or bank employees to manipulate users into providing their credentials or approving fraudulent transactions. Smishing, on the other hand, involves sending deceptive text messages containing malicious links or urgent requests, such as fake security alerts requiring immediate account verification. As mobile communication becomes more prevalent, attackers increasingly use these tactics to bypass traditional email security measures and directly target individuals.

Modern phishing campaigns have also evolved to bypass multi-factor authentication (MFA) defenses. Attackers use real-time phishing proxies that intercept MFA tokens as they are entered by victims. These proxies act as intermediaries between the user and the legitimate authentication service, capturing both the username-password combination and the temporary authentication code. By immediately replaying the stolen credentials, attackers can access the victim's account before the MFA token expires. This technique highlights the importance of implementing phishing-resistant MFA solutions, such as FIDO2 security keys or biometric authentication, which cannot be intercepted or replayed.

Another growing phishing technique is OAuth token theft, where attackers trick users into granting malicious applications access to their accounts. Instead of requesting passwords, attackers create fake OAuth consent pages that request permissions for email access, cloud storage, or administrative controls. Once a user authorizes the malicious application, attackers gain persistent access to their data and accounts without needing to steal credentials directly. Because OAuth tokens can remain valid for extended periods, they provide attackers with a stealthy method to exploit identities without triggering password resets or authentication alerts.

Phishing attacks are also frequently used to deploy malware that enables identity exploitation. Attackers send emails containing malicious attachments or embedded scripts that, when opened, install keyloggers, remote access Trojans (RATs), or credential-stealing malware on the victim's device. These malicious tools capture login credentials, monitor user activity, and allow attackers to manipulate authentication sessions. Some phishing campaigns specifically target privileged users, such as IT administrators, to obtain high-level credentials that can be used for further exploitation. Organizations must implement endpoint protection solutions, email sandboxing, and security awareness training to reduce the risks of malware-based phishing attacks.

One of the most dangerous consequences of phishing-driven identity exploitation is account takeovers (ATOs). Once attackers gain control of a user's account, they can impersonate the victim, modify account settings, and escalate privileges. In enterprise environments, compromised accounts are often used for further phishing attacks against colleagues, leveraging trust relationships to spread access within the organization. Attackers may also manipulate authentication recovery settings, such as changing backup email addresses or security questions, to maintain long-term access. Security teams must implement continuous monitoring, anomaly detection, and behavior analytics to detect and respond to ATO incidents before significant damage occurs.

To defend against phishing and identity exploitation, organizations must adopt a multi-layered security approach. Security awareness training is essential for educating employees on how to recognize phishing attempts, verify suspicious communications, and report potential attacks. Organizations should conduct simulated phishing exercises to reinforce training and assess user susceptibility to phishing tactics.

Email security measures, such as advanced spam filtering, domain authentication protocols (DMARC, SPF, and DKIM), and AI-based anomaly detection, help prevent phishing emails from reaching end users. Endpoint detection and response (EDR) solutions provide additional protection by detecting and blocking malware delivered through phishing campaigns.

Zero Trust security principles also play a crucial role in mitigating identity exploitation. By enforcing continuous authentication, least-privilege access, and adaptive risk-based authentication, organizations can reduce the impact of compromised credentials. If a phishing attack successfully steals a user's login information, Zero Trust mechanisms ensure that the attacker cannot freely move within the network without additional verification.

Threat intelligence integration further enhances phishing defense by identifying known phishing domains, tracking credential leaks, and blocking access to malicious websites. Organizations should leverage real-time threat intelligence feeds to update security policies and prevent employees from accessing phishing sites.

By combining strong authentication methods, behavioral analytics, and security awareness initiatives, organizations can significantly reduce the risks of phishing-driven identity exploitation. As attackers continue to refine their techniques, proactive defense strategies and continuous monitoring will be essential to protecting digital identities from compromise.

Dark Web Marketplaces for Stolen Identities

The dark web has become a thriving underground economy for cybercriminals looking to buy and sell stolen identities. Unlike the surface web, which is indexed and accessible through standard browsers, the dark web operates on encrypted networks such as Tor and I2P, allowing users to remain anonymous. Within these hidden marketplaces, stolen personal and corporate identities are traded for cryptocurrency, fueling a wide range of cybercrimes, including financial fraud, identity theft, account takeovers, and corporate espionage. Understanding how these marketplaces operate and the types of stolen identity data available is crucial for organizations seeking to protect themselves against identity-related threats.

Dark web marketplaces function similarly to legitimate e-commerce platforms, offering search features, customer reviews, escrow services, and even dispute resolution mechanisms. Vendors on these marketplaces sell stolen identities in various forms, including complete identity profiles, login credentials, credit card information, and authentication tokens. Some sellers specialize in providing fresh breaches, while others offer bulk databases of previously leaked information. These stolen identities are often categorized based on their level of detail, geographic location, or financial value, with high-quality credentials fetching higher prices.

One of the most sought-after items on dark web marketplaces is full identity packages, often referred to as "fullz." These packages contain an individual's personally identifiable information (PII), including full name, date of birth, Social Security number, home address, phone number, and financial details. Fullz are particularly valuable for cybercriminals engaging in financial fraud, as they allow attackers to apply for loans, open bank accounts, and conduct transactions under a victim's identity. Criminals often combine fullz with synthetic identity fraud techniques, creating entirely new identities by mixing real and fake information to bypass identity verification systems.

Corporate credentials are also highly valuable in dark web marketplaces, particularly for attackers looking to infiltrate organizations. Cybercriminals sell login credentials for corporate email accounts, virtual private networks (VPNs), cloud services, and internal business applications. These credentials are typically obtained through phishing attacks, credential stuffing, or malware infections. Once purchased, attackers can use them for business email compromise (BEC), lateral movement within corporate networks, and exfiltration of sensitive data. High-ranking executive accounts, also known as "CEO fullz" or "VIP accounts," command premium prices due to their potential for high-impact fraud and insider access.

Banking and financial institution credentials are among the most expensive commodities in dark web identity markets. Fraudsters purchase stolen bank login details to conduct unauthorized transactions, initiate wire transfers, or withdraw funds using automated teller machine (ATM) schemes. Some cybercriminals specialize in bypassing multi-factor authentication (MFA) by providing one-time passcodes obtained through social engineering, SIM swapping, or compromised authentication apps. Criminal groups often employ money mules to launder stolen funds, making it difficult for financial institutions to trace fraudulent transactions.

Ransomware groups and cyber extortionists also exploit dark web identity marketplaces to enhance their attacks. Some groups purchase administrator credentials to gain initial access to corporate environments, while others buy stolen employee directories to conduct targeted phishing campaigns. Identity-related data is often combined with other cybercriminal services, such as exploit kits, remote access tools, and botnets, to launch coordinated attacks against high-value targets. Some ransomware operators even maintain private access markets where attackers bid on compromised corporate networks, with the highest bidder gaining exclusive control over the victim's infrastructure.

Healthcare identity data is another valuable commodity in dark web markets, often surpassing the price of financial credentials. Medical records contain a wealth of personal information that can be used for insurance fraud, prescription fraud, and medical identity theft. Unlike credit card data, which can be deactivated once compromised, medical records are permanent and cannot be easily changed. Cybercriminals use stolen healthcare identities to obtain expensive medical treatments, purchase prescription drugs, and file fraudulent insurance claims. The long-term impact of healthcare identity theft makes it particularly difficult for victims to recover from such fraud.

Government-issued identity documents, such as passports, driver's licenses, and national ID cards, are frequently traded in dark web marketplaces. Attackers use these documents to create counterfeit identities, facilitate human trafficking, and evade law enforcement detection. Some dark web vendors offer high-quality forged documents with matching biometric data, allowing criminals to bypass border security and identity verification checks. The availability of these fraudulent documents poses a significant threat to national security, enabling criminals and terrorists to operate under false identities.

One of the key drivers of dark web identity trading is the growing number of data breaches that expose millions of credentials and personal records each year. Once a breach occurs, cybercriminals quickly compile and sell the stolen data in underground forums. Some breaches lead to the creation of "combo lists," massive databases of usernames and passwords aggregated from multiple breaches. Attackers use these lists in automated credential stuffing attacks, testing stolen credentials against various online services in the hopes that users have reused their passwords. Organizations that fail to enforce strong authentication practices are particularly vulnerable to these attacks.

Dark web monitoring has become an essential tool for cybersecurity teams looking to protect their organizations from identity-related threats. Many security vendors offer dark web intelligence services that continuously scan underground forums and marketplaces for stolen credentials linked to corporate domains. When compromised credentials are detected, organizations can take proactive measures such as enforcing password resets, enabling MFA, and revoking access to compromised accounts. Threat intelligence feeds also provide insights into emerging trends in identity fraud, allowing organizations to adapt their security strategies accordingly.

Despite efforts to disrupt dark web marketplaces through law enforcement actions, these platforms continue to evolve. When a major dark web marketplace is shut down, new ones quickly emerge to replace it. Some cybercriminal groups operate invitation-only markets, restricting access to vetted buyers and sellers to avoid law enforcement infiltration. Others use decentralized and encrypted communication platforms, such as Telegram and Discord, to conduct transactions outside of traditional dark web forums. These adaptations make it increasingly difficult to dismantle the underground identity economy.

To mitigate the risks associated with dark web identity trading, organizations must adopt a proactive security approach. Implementing strong password policies, enforcing MFA, and continuously monitoring identity access logs can reduce the likelihood of credential compromise. Security awareness training is also critical, as many identity breaches originate from phishing attacks and social engineering schemes. Organizations should educate employees on recognizing suspicious emails, avoiding credential reuse, and reporting potential security threats.

The dark web's role in identity exploitation underscores the need for comprehensive identity security measures. As cybercriminals continue to monetize stolen credentials and personal data, organizations and individuals must remain vigilant in protecting their digital identities. By leveraging advanced threat detection, continuous monitoring, and robust authentication practices, organizations can reduce their exposure to identity-related threats and prevent stolen credentials from being used against them.

Data Breaches and Identity Exposure

Data breaches have become one of the most significant threats to identity security, exposing sensitive personal and corporate information to cybercriminals. Organizations across all industries, from financial institutions to healthcare providers and government agencies, have fallen victim to large-scale data breaches that compromise millions of identities. Once this data is leaked, it can be used for financial fraud, identity theft, credential stuffing attacks, and corporate espionage. The consequences of data breaches extend beyond immediate financial losses, often leading to reputational damage, regulatory penalties, and long-term security risks.

The primary cause of data breaches is unauthorized access to sensitive databases. Attackers exploit vulnerabilities in web applications, cloud storage, and internal networks to extract valuable data, including usernames, passwords, email addresses, Social Security numbers, and payment card information. Many breaches occur due to weak authentication mechanisms, misconfigured security settings, and poor access control policies. Once attackers gain entry, they exfiltrate data in bulk and often sell it on dark web marketplaces, where other cybercriminals use it for various identity-based attacks.

One of the most alarming aspects of data breaches is the exposure of login credentials. Many users reuse passwords across multiple online services, which allows attackers to leverage stolen credentials in credential stuffing attacks. These attacks involve automated scripts that test stolen username-password pairs against various websites in an attempt to gain unauthorized access. If a user's credentials from one breached website match their login information on another platform, attackers can easily take over multiple accounts. This risk highlights the importance of using unique passwords for every account and enabling multi-factor authentication (MFA) to reduce the effectiveness of stolen credentials.

The financial sector is a frequent target of data breaches due to the high value of banking credentials and credit card information. Attackers who obtain financial data can engage in fraudulent transactions, apply for loans under a victim's name, or sell the stolen information on underground forums. Credit card information is particularly lucrative, with cybercriminals often selling "carding" details that include card numbers, expiration dates, CVVs, and billing addresses. Some fraudsters use stolen financial data to create cloned credit cards or conduct unauthorized purchases before cardholders detect the fraud.

Healthcare organizations also face significant risks from data breaches, as medical records contain extensive personal information that can be exploited for fraud. Unlike credit card numbers, which can be canceled and replaced, medical records are permanent and cannot be easily changed. Attackers use stolen healthcare data to file fraudulent insurance claims, obtain prescription medications, and access medical services under a victim's identity. This type of identity theft can have long-term consequences, as fraudulent medical records may lead to incorrect treatments or billing issues for the real patient.

Government agencies are another prime target for data breaches, as they store vast amounts of personally identifiable information (PII), including tax records, driver's licenses, and passport details. When such data is exposed, cybercriminals can create synthetic identities—combinations of real and fake information used to bypass identity verification systems. Synthetic identity fraud is particularly difficult to detect because it does not rely on stolen credit cards or bank accounts but instead builds entirely new identities that can be used for long-term fraud.

Corporate breaches often result in the exposure of employee credentials, internal emails, intellectual property, and confidential business data. Attackers who gain access to corporate identity systems can escalate privileges, access sensitive documents, and conduct business email compromise (BEC) scams. In many cases, stolen employee credentials are used to impersonate executives or finance personnel, tricking employees into wiring money to fraudulent accounts. The exposure of internal communications and trade secrets can also give competitors an unfair advantage or lead to legal complications.

Cloud security misconfigurations are a growing cause of data breaches and identity exposure. Many organizations store vast amounts of sensitive information in cloud environments, but failing to properly configure identity access policies can leave data exposed to unauthorized access. Publicly accessible cloud storage buckets, weak API authentication, and excessive permissions often result in large-scale breaches that expose corporate and customer data. Organizations must implement strict access controls, encrypt sensitive data, and continuously monitor cloud environments for misconfigurations to prevent unauthorized access.

The impact of data breaches extends far beyond the initial attack. Once personal or corporate data is exposed, it often remains available indefinitely on the dark web, where cybercriminals can repurpose it for future attacks. Even if a breached organization quickly resets passwords and enhances security, previously stolen data may still be exploited in phishing campaigns, identity fraud, and account takeovers. Security teams must implement continuous monitoring and dark web intelligence to detect and mitigate threats stemming from past breaches.

Regulatory compliance plays a crucial role in mitigating the risks associated with data breaches. Many jurisdictions have enacted strict data protection laws, such as the General Data Protection Regulation (GDPR) in Europe and the California Consumer Privacy Act (CCPA) in the United States. These regulations require organizations to implement strong data protection measures, notify affected individuals in the event of a breach, and impose significant fines for non-compliance. Organizations must ensure they adhere to regulatory requirements by encrypting sensitive data, conducting regular security audits, and maintaining robust incident response plans.

Incident response planning is essential for minimizing the damage caused by data breaches. Organizations must have predefined protocols for detecting, containing, and remediating breaches, including steps for notifying affected users, working with law enforcement, and securing compromised systems. Automated response mechanisms, such as temporarily locking affected accounts and forcing password resets, can help mitigate the immediate impact of a breach. Security teams should also conduct post-incident reviews to identify vulnerabilities that led to the breach and implement measures to prevent future incidents.

Employee training and security awareness programs are critical components of a strong data breach prevention strategy. Many breaches result from human error, such as falling for phishing emails, using weak passwords, or misconfiguring security settings. Organizations must educate employees on best practices for identity security, including recognizing social engineering attempts, securely handling sensitive data, and reporting suspicious activity. Regular security drills and phishing simulations help reinforce these lessons and reduce the risk of accidental data exposure.

To protect against data breaches and identity exposure, organizations must adopt a multi-layered security approach. This includes implementing robust identity and access management (IAM) solutions, enforcing least-privilege access policies, monitoring authentication logs for anomalies, and leveraging artificial intelligence (AI) to detect suspicious behavior. Advanced threat detection solutions, such as Security Information and Event Management (SIEM) and User and Entity Behavior Analytics (UEBA), help identify early signs of identity compromise before a full-scale breach occurs.

By understanding the risks associated with data breaches and proactively strengthening identity security measures, organizations can reduce their exposure to cyber threats and better protect sensitive information. In an era where data breaches have become a persistent and evolving challenge, continuous vigilance and adaptive security strategies are essential for mitigating the impact of identity exposure.

Mitigating Identity Risks in Third-Party Access

Third-party access is a critical component of modern business operations, enabling organizations to collaborate with vendors, contractors, service providers, and business partners. However, granting external entities access to internal systems introduces significant identity security risks. Many high-profile data breaches and cyberattacks have originated from compromised third-party accounts, as attackers often exploit weaker security practices within supply chains to infiltrate larger targets. Mitigating identity risks in third-party access requires a combination of strict access controls, continuous monitoring, and robust authentication mechanisms to ensure that external identities do not become security vulnerabilities.

One of the primary risks associated with third-party access is overprivileged accounts. Many organizations grant external users broad access to systems, often exceeding what is necessary for their specific tasks. Attackers who compromise third-party credentials can exploit these excessive permissions to move laterally within an organization, escalate privileges, and exfiltrate sensitive data. To mitigate this risk, organizations should enforce the principle of least privilege (PoLP), ensuring that third-party users have only the minimum level of access required for their roles. Access reviews should be conducted regularly to identify and remove unnecessary permissions.

Multi-factor authentication (MFA) is a crucial defense against identity compromise in third-party access. Many cybercriminals target third-party accounts because they often lack strong authentication protections. Implementing mandatory MFA for all external users significantly reduces the risk of credential-based attacks. Organizations should prioritize phishing-resistant MFA methods, such as FIDO2 security keys or biometric authentication, to prevent attackers from bypassing authentication through phishing or real-time credential theft.

Another critical security measure is the use of just-in-time (JIT) access controls. Rather than providing third-party users with continuous access to systems, JIT access grants temporary permissions only when needed. This minimizes the attack surface by ensuring that credentials are not left exposed for extended periods. Automated approval workflows can further enhance security by requiring validation before third-party users gain access to sensitive resources.

Identity federation and Single Sign-On (SSO) solutions help streamline third-party access while maintaining security. Instead of managing separate credentials for each vendor, organizations can use federated identity management to authenticate external users through their home organizations. However, identity federation introduces risks if third-party identity providers are not adequately secured. Organizations must carefully vet third-party identity providers, enforce strong authentication policies, and continuously monitor federated access logs for signs of compromise.

Third-party service accounts and API integrations also pose significant identity security risks. Many organizations rely on external applications that require persistent access to internal systems through API keys, service accounts, or OAuth tokens. If attackers compromise these credentials, they can manipulate data, extract sensitive information, or disrupt business operations. To mitigate these risks, organizations should enforce strict API security controls, regularly rotate API keys, and use attribute-based access control (ABAC) to limit what external applications can access. Continuous monitoring of API activity helps detect anomalies that could indicate credential abuse.

Regular identity risk assessments for third-party access are essential for maintaining security. Organizations should conduct periodic audits to evaluate the security posture of vendors and external partners, ensuring they adhere to best practices for identity management. Vendor security questionnaires, penetration testing, and compliance certifications can help assess the risk levels of third-party entities. Contracts and service-level agreements (SLAs) should include security requirements, such as mandatory MFA enforcement, regular security training for third-party employees, and prompt notification of any security incidents.

Monitoring third-party access in real-time is critical for detecting identity threats. Security teams should implement Security Information and Event Management (SIEM) solutions that aggregate identity-related events, including authentication attempts, privilege escalations, and access anomalies. User and Entity Behavior Analytics (UEBA) can help identify suspicious activity by analyzing deviations from normal third-party behavior. If a vendor account suddenly accesses systems outside its usual scope or logs in from an unusual location, security teams can investigate and respond before an incident escalates.

Zero Trust security models provide a comprehensive approach to mitigating identity risks in third-party access. Unlike traditional perimeter-based security, Zero Trust assumes that no user—internal or external—should be trusted by default. Every access request is verified based on identity, device health, risk level, and behavioral patterns. Implementing Zero Trust principles ensures that third-party users undergo continuous authentication and authorization, reducing the likelihood of credential misuse.

Incident response planning must account for third-party identity compromises. Organizations should have predefined workflows for revoking access, resetting credentials, and investigating potential breaches involving third-party users. Automated response mechanisms, such as disabling accounts after detecting anomalous behavior, can help contain threats before they cause significant damage. Security teams should also establish direct communication channels with vendors to coordinate rapid response efforts in case of a security incident.

Continuous security awareness training for both internal employees and third-party users is essential for reducing identity risks. Many identity-related breaches stem from human error, such as falling for phishing attacks or mishandling credentials. Organizations should educate third-party users on secure authentication practices, recognizing phishing attempts, and following security policies. Phishing simulation exercises and periodic security briefings can reinforce these lessons and help prevent identity compromise.

Dark web monitoring can provide early warnings of third-party identity risks. If a vendor's credentials appear in a data breach or are listed for sale on underground forums, organizations can take proactive measures, such as forcing password resets and enforcing additional authentication requirements. Threat intelligence platforms that track credential leaks and identity fraud trends can help organizations stay ahead of emerging threats.

To further enhance security, organizations should implement access expiration policies for third-party users. Many external accounts remain active long after a vendor's engagement ends, creating unnecessary security risks. Organizations should enforce automatic account deactivation after a predefined period of inactivity. Regular access recertification processes help ensure that only active and authorized third-party users retain access to critical systems.

By implementing strong authentication mechanisms, enforcing least privilege access, continuously monitoring identity activity, and integrating Zero Trust principles, organizations can mitigate the identity risks associated with third-party access. As supply chain threats and vendor-related breaches continue to rise, proactive identity security measures are essential for safeguarding sensitive systems and preventing unauthorized access.

Automating Identity Threat Response

As cyber threats targeting identities become more sophisticated, organizations must adopt automation to detect, respond to, and mitigate identity-related security incidents in real time. Manual threat response processes often fall short in addressing modern identity attacks, as they require significant time and resources, leaving organizations vulnerable to credential compromise, privilege escalation, and lateral movement. Automating identity threat response enhances security operations by reducing response times, minimizing human error, and ensuring consistent enforcement of security policies. By integrating automation with identity and access management (IAM) systems, security information and event management (SIEM) platforms, and identity threat detection and response (ITDR) solutions, organizations can build a proactive and resilient identity security framework.

One of the most effective ways to automate identity threat response is through the implementation of Security Orchestration, Automation, and Response (SOAR) platforms. SOAR solutions integrate with existing security tools, such as SIEM, IAM, and endpoint detection and response (EDR) platforms, to orchestrate automated responses based on predefined security workflows. When an identity-related security event is detected—such as an account takeover attempt, unusual authentication behavior, or unauthorized privilege escalation—SOAR systems can automatically trigger response actions, such as disabling compromised accounts, enforcing password resets, and revoking access tokens. By automating these responses, organizations can contain identity threats before they escalate into full-scale breaches.

Automated anomaly detection plays a crucial role in identity threat response. User and Entity Behavior Analytics (UEBA) solutions leverage machine learning to establish baselines of normal user behavior and detect deviations that may indicate identity compromise. For example, if a user who typically logs in from a corporate office suddenly attempts to access systems from an unfamiliar country, UEBA can flag this anomaly and trigger automated risk-based authentication measures. If the risk level is high, the system can enforce step-up authentication, requiring additional verification before granting access. By integrating UEBA with automated response mechanisms, organizations can dynamically adjust security policies based on real-time risk assessments.

Identity lifecycle management automation is another key component of identity threat response. Organizations often struggle with managing user accounts, particularly when employees change roles, leave the company, or contractors complete their assignments. If inactive or orphaned accounts remain in the system, attackers can exploit them to gain unauthorized access. Automating identity lifecycle management ensures that accounts are deactivated when no longer needed, access permissions are adjusted based on role changes, and periodic access reviews are conducted without manual intervention. Identity governance and administration (IGA) solutions streamline this process by enforcing automated policies for account provisioning, deprovisioning, and recertification.

Privileged access management (PAM) solutions also benefit from automation by enforcing just-in-time (JIT) privilege elevation and session monitoring. Traditional privileged accounts present a significant security risk, as attackers often target administrative credentials to gain full control over systems. Automating privileged access controls ensures that users receive elevated privileges only when necessary and for a limited duration. If an attacker attempts to escalate privileges or access sensitive resources outside of normal patterns, automated responses can immediately terminate the session, revoke privileges, and alert security teams for further investigation.

Multi-factor authentication (MFA) response automation is critical for mitigating identity threats. Attackers frequently target authentication processes through phishing, credential stuffing, and MFA fatigue attacks. Automated security workflows can detect multiple failed authentication attempts, unusual MFA resets, or changes in authentication methods and take immediate action. For example, if a user suddenly switches from biometric authentication to SMS-based MFA, the system can require additional verification before allowing the change. Automating these responses helps prevent attackers from bypassing MFA protections and taking over user accounts.

API security automation is essential for protecting machine identities and service accounts, which are increasingly targeted in identity-based attacks. Many cloud services and third-party applications rely on API keys, OAuth tokens, and service credentials for authentication. If these credentials are leaked or misused, attackers can manipulate cloud resources, extract sensitive data, or execute unauthorized actions. Automated API security solutions continuously monitor API traffic, detect anomalies such as excessive API calls from unknown sources, and revoke compromised tokens in real time. By integrating API security with identity threat response automation, organizations can prevent unauthorized access to cloud environments.

Automated response to credential exposure on the dark web enhances identity protection by proactively identifying compromised accounts before they are exploited. Threat intelligence platforms that monitor underground forums, breach databases, and credential dumps can integrate with IAM and ITDR solutions to trigger automated security measures when stolen credentials are detected. If an employee's corporate credentials appear in a data breach, automated workflows can enforce an immediate password reset, require additional authentication steps, and notify security teams for further investigation. This proactive approach minimizes the risk of credential-based attacks.

Incident response playbooks are essential for defining automated identity threat response workflows. Organizations should develop standardized response procedures for common identity-related security incidents, such as phishing attacks, insider threats, and unauthorized access attempts. These playbooks should specify automated actions, such as isolating compromised accounts, revoking access permissions, and logging forensic data for further analysis. By automating incident response playbooks through SOAR platforms, security teams can ensure consistent and efficient execution of identity threat mitigation strategies.

Compliance and audit automation strengthens identity security by ensuring adherence to regulatory requirements and security best practices. Many data protection laws, such as GDPR, CCPA, and HIPAA, mandate strict identity security controls, including access reviews, authentication policies, and user activity logging. Automating compliance monitoring enables organizations to generate real-time reports, detect policy violations, and enforce corrective actions without manual effort. Automated identity auditing tools can continuously scan access logs, detect unauthorized privilege changes, and ensure that security policies are consistently applied across all identity systems.

Continuous monitoring and self-healing identity security systems represent the next stage of automation in identity threat response. AI-driven security solutions can autonomously detect and respond to threats, adjusting security policies in real time based on evolving attack patterns. For example, if an attacker repeatedly attempts to brute-force a set of credentials, an AI-driven system can dynamically adjust rate-limiting rules, block the attacker's IP address, and require step-up authentication for affected accounts. By leveraging AI-powered automation, organizations can create adaptive identity security frameworks that respond to threats in real time.

Automating identity threat response does not eliminate the need for human oversight. Security teams should continuously refine automated workflows, analyze response effectiveness, and fine-tune detection models to reduce false positives and improve accuracy. Automated solutions should complement human expertise, allowing analysts to focus on high-priority investigations and strategic security initiatives.

By integrating automated identity threat response across IAM, SIEM, UEBA, PAM, and SOAR platforms, organizations can significantly enhance their ability to detect and mitigate identity-related threats in real time. Automated security measures reduce response times, minimize manual intervention, and strengthen overall identity protection, ensuring that organizations remain resilient against evolving cyber threats.

Identity Governance and Risk Management

Identity governance and risk management are fundamental components of a strong cybersecurity framework, ensuring that user identities are managed, monitored, and secured across an organization. As businesses expand their digital footprint, the number of user accounts, privileged identities, and access permissions continues to grow, increasing the risk of unauthorized access, insider threats, and compliance violations. Without proper governance, organizations face significant security challenges, including excessive privileges, orphaned accounts, and identity-based attacks. A well-structured identity governance and risk management strategy helps organizations enforce security policies, reduce risks, and maintain compliance with regulatory standards.

One of the key aspects of identity governance is access control. Organizations must ensure that employees, contractors, and third-party vendors have the appropriate level of access based on their roles and responsibilities. Role-Based Access Control (RBAC) is a common approach that assigns access permissions based on predefined job functions, reducing the risk of unauthorized access. However, RBAC alone is not always sufficient, as roles can evolve over time, leading to privilege creep. To mitigate this risk, organizations should implement Attribute-Based Access Control (ABAC), which evaluates additional factors such as device security, location, and time of access before granting permissions.

Access reviews and certification play a crucial role in identity governance. Periodic access reviews help organizations validate whether users still require the permissions they have been granted. Managers and security teams should regularly review user access rights, revoking unnecessary privileges and deactivating inactive accounts. Automated identity governance solutions streamline this process by generating reports on access anomalies, flagging excessive permissions, and enforcing policy-driven corrective actions. Access certification ensures that only authorized users maintain access to sensitive resources, reducing the risk of insider threats and compliance violations.

Risk-based identity management enhances governance by prioritizing security controls based on the potential impact of identity-related threats. Not all user accounts pose the same level of risk—privileged accounts, administrative identities, and service accounts represent higher security risks compared to standard employee accounts. Organizations should implement risk scoring models that assess the likelihood and impact of identity threats based on user behavior, authentication patterns, and access history. High-risk accounts should be subject to stricter security measures, including continuous authentication, just-in-time privilege elevation, and enhanced monitoring.

Privileged access management (PAM) is an essential component of identity risk management. Privileged accounts, such as system administrators, database managers, and cloud operators, have elevated access rights that make them attractive targets for cybercriminals. If compromised, these accounts can be used to disable security controls, exfiltrate data, and deploy ransomware. PAM solutions enforce strict controls over privileged access by requiring just-in-time (JIT) privilege elevation, session recording, and real-time activity monitoring. By limiting the exposure of privileged accounts and enforcing least privilege access, organizations can significantly reduce the risk of identity-based attacks.

Identity governance also extends to third-party risk management. Many organizations rely on external vendors, contractors, and service providers that require access to corporate systems. Without proper oversight, third-party accounts can become security blind spots, increasing the risk of supply chain attacks. Organizations should enforce strict access controls for third-party users, including mandatory multi-factor authentication (MFA), time-limited access permissions, and continuous monitoring of third-party activities. Identity governance frameworks should include vendor security assessments, ensuring that external partners adhere to the same identity security standards as internal users.

Automated identity lifecycle management is a critical aspect of identity governance, reducing the risk of orphaned accounts and unauthorized access. User accounts should be automatically provisioned when employees join an organization, updated when they change roles, and deprovisioned when they leave. Many security breaches occur because inactive accounts are not properly disabled, allowing attackers to exploit them for unauthorized access. Identity governance platforms integrate with human resources (HR) systems to ensure that access permissions are dynamically updated based on employment status, reducing the risk of identity misuse.

Data governance is closely linked to identity governance, as unauthorized access to sensitive data can lead to compliance violations and security breaches. Organizations must classify and protect data based on sensitivity levels, implementing access controls that restrict data access to authorized users. Identity governance solutions integrate with data protection technologies, such as encryption, data loss prevention (DLP), and audit logging, to ensure that user identities interact with data securely. By correlating identity governance with data security policies, organizations can prevent unauthorized access, data exfiltration, and regulatory non-compliance.

Regulatory compliance is a major driver of identity governance initiatives, as organizations must adhere to industry standards and data protection laws. Regulations such as the General Data Protection Regulation (GDPR), the California Consumer Privacy Act (CCPA), and the Health Insurance Portability and Accountability Act (HIPAA) impose strict identity management requirements, including access controls, user activity monitoring, and data protection measures. Failure to comply with these regulations can result in legal penalties, financial fines, and reputational damage. Identity governance frameworks help organizations demonstrate compliance by maintaining audit trails, enforcing security policies, and generating compliance reports.

Identity governance platforms leverage artificial intelligence (AI) and machine learning (ML) to enhance security and automate decision-making. AI-driven identity governance solutions analyze user behavior, detect anomalies, and recommend policy adjustments to reduce risk. For example, if a user frequently accesses high-risk systems outside of business hours, AI algorithms can flag this behavior as suspicious and trigger an access review. ML-powered identity analytics also help organizations predict potential identity threats based on historical data, enabling proactive risk mitigation strategies.

Zero Trust security models align closely with identity governance principles, ensuring that access decisions are based on continuous verification rather than static trust assumptions. Zero Trust frameworks enforce strict identity verification at every stage of access, evaluating contextual risk factors such as device security, geolocation, and authentication history. By integrating Zero Trust principles into identity governance strategies, organizations can enhance security, prevent unauthorized access, and reduce reliance on perimeter-based defenses.

Incident response and identity governance must work together to mitigate identity-related security breaches. Organizations should establish automated response workflows that detect and contain identity threats in real time. If an identity compromise is detected—such as an account takeover or unauthorized privilege escalation—automated security policies can disable affected accounts, enforce password resets, and trigger forensic investigations. Security teams should also conduct post-incident reviews to assess identity governance gaps and strengthen access controls based on lessons learned from security incidents.

Identity governance and risk management are ongoing processes that require continuous monitoring, policy enforcement, and adaptation to emerging threats. By implementing strong identity governance frameworks, organizations can minimize security risks, enforce least privilege access, and ensure compliance with regulatory requirements. Effective identity governance not only protects user identities but also strengthens overall cybersecurity resilience, reducing the likelihood of identity-related breaches and financial losses.

Role-Based Access Control vs. Attribute-Based Access Control

Access control is a fundamental aspect of identity security, ensuring that users have the appropriate level of access to systems, applications, and data. Organizations must implement access control mechanisms to protect sensitive information, enforce security policies, and comply with regulatory requirements. Two of the most widely used models for access control are Role-Based Access Control (RBAC) and Attribute-Based Access Control (ABAC). While both approaches aim to regulate user access based on predefined rules, they differ in how they define access permissions, manage user roles, and adapt to dynamic security environments. Understanding the differences between RBAC and ABAC is essential for organizations seeking to implement effective access control strategies.

Role-Based Access Control (RBAC) is one of the most commonly used access control models in enterprise environments. In RBAC, access permissions are assigned to users based on their roles within an organization. Each role defines a set of permissions that determine what actions a user can perform within a system. For example, a finance department employee may be assigned a "Financial Analyst" role, which grants access to accounting software, financial reports, and budgeting tools. Similarly, an IT administrator role may have elevated privileges to configure system settings and manage user accounts. By grouping users into roles, RBAC simplifies access management and reduces administrative overhead.

One of the main advantages of RBAC is its ease of implementation and scalability. Organizations can define a limited number of roles that align with job functions and assign users to these roles based on their responsibilities. This approach eliminates the need to assign permissions on an individual basis, making access management more efficient. Additionally, RBAC supports the principle of least privilege by ensuring that users receive only the permissions necessary for their roles. When an employee changes roles or leaves the organization, access rights can be easily modified or revoked by updating role assignments.

Despite its advantages, RBAC has limitations in dynamic and complex environments. One of the key challenges is role explosion, where organizations create too many roles to accommodate varying access needs. As businesses evolve, new job functions emerge, and access requirements change, leading to an overwhelming number of roles that become difficult to manage. Another limitation is RBAC's static nature—access decisions are based solely on predefined roles and do not take contextual factors into account. For example, RBAC cannot enforce access restrictions based on factors such as device security, location, or time of access, which are critical for modern security policies.

Attribute-Based Access Control (ABAC) addresses the limitations of RBAC by using a more dynamic and flexible approach to access management. Instead of relying solely on roles, ABAC evaluates attributes—such as user identity, job function, location, device type, and security clearance—to determine access permissions. In ABAC, access decisions are based on a set of policies that define how attributes interact. For example, a policy might state that only users with the "Manager" job title can access financial reports, but access is restricted if they are logging in from an untrusted device or outside of business hours.

One of the key benefits of ABAC is its ability to provide fine-grained access control. Organizations can create highly specific access policies that consider multiple factors, ensuring that users receive the appropriate level of access based on contextual conditions. This approach enhances security by reducing the risk of unauthorized access and insider threats. For instance, an organization may enforce a policy that prevents employees from accessing sensitive customer data unless they are on a corporate network and using an endpoint that meets security compliance standards. By incorporating these contextual factors, ABAC offers greater control over access decisions compared to RBAC.

Another advantage of ABAC is its adaptability to changing security requirements. Unlike RBAC, which requires manual role updates when access needs change, ABAC dynamically evaluates access requests based on real-time conditions. This makes ABAC particularly useful in cloud environments, where users access resources from different locations and devices. Security policies in ABAC can be updated without modifying individual user permissions, ensuring that access controls remain aligned with evolving security policies and compliance mandates.

However, implementing ABAC can be more complex than RBAC due to the need for detailed policy definitions and attribute management. Organizations must define and maintain a comprehensive set of attributes, ensuring that data sources used for access decisions are accurate and up to date. Additionally, ABAC requires a policy engine capable of evaluating multiple attributes and making real-time access decisions, which may introduce performance considerations in high-volume environments. Despite these challenges, the flexibility and precision of ABAC make it a powerful solution for organizations that require dynamic access control.

Choosing between RBAC and ABAC depends on the specific needs of an organization. RBAC is well-suited for environments where job functions and access requirements are relatively stable, making it a practical choice for organizations with well-defined role structures. It is easy to implement, reduces administrative overhead, and supports regulatory compliance by enforcing consistent access policies. However, for organizations that require more granular access control, dynamic policy enforcement, and context-aware security, ABAC provides a more sophisticated approach that adapts to modern security challenges.

Many organizations adopt a hybrid approach that combines RBAC and ABAC to leverage the strengths of both models. In this approach, RBAC is used as a baseline to define general access permissions based on job roles, while ABAC is layered on top to enforce additional security controls based on attributes. For example, a user may be granted access to an application based on their RBAC role, but ABAC policies can further restrict access based on real-time factors such as location, risk level, and device compliance. This hybrid model enhances security while maintaining the simplicity of role-based management.

As identity security threats continue to evolve, organizations must carefully evaluate their access control strategies to ensure that they balance security, usability, and operational efficiency. Whether adopting RBAC, ABAC, or a combination of both, organizations should continuously review and refine their access control policies to align with business needs and emerging security risks. By implementing a well-structured access control framework, organizations can protect sensitive data, prevent unauthorized access, and strengthen overall identity security.

Identity Threats in IoT and OT Environments

The proliferation of Internet of Things (IoT) and Operational Technology (OT) devices has introduced significant identity security challenges across various industries. These devices, ranging from smart sensors and industrial control systems to medical equipment and smart home devices, often operate with weak authentication mechanisms, making them prime targets for cybercriminals. Unlike traditional IT systems, IoT and OT environments frequently lack strong identity and access management (IAM) controls, exposing them to identity-based threats such as unauthorized access, device impersonation, privilege escalation, and lateral movement. As these environments become increasingly interconnected, securing identities within IoT and OT networks is essential for preventing cyberattacks and maintaining operational integrity.

One of the most critical identity threats in IoT and OT environments is the use of weak or hardcoded credentials. Many IoT and OT devices come with factory-default usernames and passwords that are rarely changed after deployment. Attackers exploit these default credentials to gain unauthorized access, often leveraging automated scanning tools to identify vulnerable devices on the network. Once compromised, these devices can be used as entry points for further attacks, including data exfiltration, network reconnaissance, and ransomware deployment. Organizations must enforce strict credential management policies, requiring unique passwords for each device and integrating them into centralized IAM systems.

Another significant threat is the lack of multi-factor authentication (MFA) in IoT and OT environments. While MFA has become a standard security measure in traditional IT systems, many IoT and OT devices do not support advanced authentication mechanisms. Without MFA, attackers can easily hijack device credentials through phishing, credential stuffing, or brute-force attacks. Even when MFA is available, organizations often fail to implement it consistently across all devices. To mitigate this risk, security teams should prioritize IoT and OT devices that support MFA and explore alternative authentication methods, such as certificate-based authentication and hardware security tokens.

Device impersonation and spoofing present additional identity threats in IoT and OT networks. Attackers can manipulate or clone legitimate devices to bypass authentication controls and gain access to critical infrastructure. For example, in industrial environments, attackers may spoof a sensor or controller to send falsified data, disrupting operations and causing financial losses. Similarly, in healthcare settings, attackers could impersonate medical devices to interfere with patient monitoring systems. Implementing cryptographic authentication and secure identity verification for IoT and OT devices helps prevent impersonation attacks and ensures that only legitimate devices communicate within the network.

Privilege escalation is a common tactic used by attackers in IoT and OT environments. Many devices operate with excessive privileges, allowing attackers to exploit vulnerabilities and gain administrative access. Once an attacker escalates privileges, they can modify device configurations, disable security controls, and spread malware throughout the network. Organizations must enforce the principle of least privilege (PoLP) by restricting device permissions to only the necessary level required for their intended function. Role-based access control (RBAC) and attribute-based access control (ABAC) can further enhance identity security by limiting access based on user roles, device attributes, and contextual factors.

Lateral movement is another critical concern in IoT and OT environments. Once attackers gain access to a single compromised device, they often attempt to move laterally across the network to infiltrate more valuable assets. Many IoT and OT networks lack proper segmentation, allowing attackers to pivot from low-security devices to high-value targets, such as industrial control systems, surveillance cameras, or data storage servers. Implementing network segmentation and Zero Trust security models can help contain threats by restricting device-to-device communication and continuously verifying identity and access requests.

Supply chain attacks targeting IoT and OT identities have also become a growing concern. Many organizations rely on third-party vendors and manufacturers to provide IoT and OT devices, creating security blind spots. If a vendor's identity management practices are weak, attackers can compromise devices before they even reach the customer. This was evident in past supply chain attacks where malicious actors inserted backdoors into IoT firmware, allowing remote access to compromised devices. To mitigate supply chain risks, organizations should conduct security assessments of IoT and OT vendors, enforce strict firmware integrity checks, and require digital signatures for device updates.

Cloud integration further complicates identity security in IoT and OT environments. Many modern IoT devices rely on cloud services for data processing, remote management, and analytics. If cloud identity security is weak, attackers can hijack cloud-based IoT accounts, gain control over multiple devices, and manipulate their functionality. Securing IoT and OT identities in the cloud requires enforcing strong API security, implementing risk-based authentication, and continuously monitoring cloud access logs for anomalies.

Ransomware and identity threats in IoT and OT networks are becoming more prevalent. Attackers increasingly target IoT and OT devices to disrupt critical infrastructure, manufacturing plants, and healthcare facilities. Compromised devices can be locked down, rendering them unusable until a ransom is paid. In some cases, attackers gain control of OT systems and demand payment in exchange for restoring normal operations. To defend against ransomware targeting IoT and OT identities, organizations should implement automated identity threat detection, enforce strict access controls, and deploy endpoint protection solutions tailored for IoT and OT environments.

Incident response for identity threats in IoT and OT environments requires specialized strategies. Traditional IT security measures may not be directly applicable to IoT and OT devices due to their limited processing power and unique operating systems. Security teams should develop dedicated incident response playbooks that account for the distinct characteristics of IoT and OT networks. This includes automated threat containment, rapid credential revocation, and forensic analysis of compromised devices. Additionally, organizations should conduct regular security drills and penetration testing to identify and address identity vulnerabilities before attackers can exploit them.

Regulatory compliance is increasingly shaping identity security in IoT and OT environments. Governments and industry bodies have introduced security frameworks, such as the NIST Cybersecurity Framework and IEC 62443, which mandate strict identity and access management requirements for IoT and OT systems. Compliance with these standards requires organizations to implement strong authentication controls, continuous identity monitoring, and secure firmware update mechanisms. Adopting a compliance-driven approach helps organizations align their IoT and OT identity security practices with industry best practices and regulatory expectations.

The integration of artificial intelligence (AI) and machine learning (ML) is enhancing identity threat detection in IoT and OT networks. AI-driven security solutions analyze vast amounts of identity-related data, detecting anomalies and predicting potential threats before they escalate. ML algorithms can identify abnormal authentication patterns, detect unauthorized access attempts, and automatically enforce security policies. By leveraging AI and ML for identity threat detection, organizations can strengthen their ability to respond to emerging threats in IoT and OT environments.

Securing identities in IoT and OT environments requires a proactive and multi-layered approach. By enforcing strong authentication mechanisms, implementing identity governance frameworks, and continuously monitoring for identity threats, organizations can protect IoT and OT devices from unauthorized access and cyberattacks. As IoT and OT adoption continues to expand, identity security will remain a critical focus for safeguarding critical infrastructure, industrial operations, and connected environments from identity-based threats.

Legal and Compliance Considerations for Identity Security

Identity security is not only a critical component of cybersecurity but also a legal and regulatory requirement for organizations across various industries. Governments and regulatory bodies worldwide have established strict laws and standards to ensure that personal data, authentication mechanisms, and access controls are properly managed and protected. Non-compliance can result in severe financial penalties, legal consequences, reputational damage, and loss of customer trust. Organizations must align their identity security strategies with legal and compliance frameworks to mitigate risks, safeguard sensitive information, and demonstrate due diligence in identity and access management (IAM).

One of the most significant legal frameworks governing identity security is the General Data Protection Regulation (GDPR), implemented by the European Union. GDPR mandates strict identity security controls for organizations that handle the personal data of EU citizens. This regulation requires businesses to implement strong authentication, encryption, and access control measures to protect user identities. Organizations must also enforce role-based access control (RBAC) and least privilege principles to ensure that employees only access data necessary for their job functions. In the event of a data breach involving identity information, GDPR requires organizations to notify affected individuals and relevant authorities within 72 hours. Non-compliance can lead to fines of up to 4% of annual global revenue or €20 million, whichever is higher.

In the United States, the California Consumer Privacy Act (CCPA) establishes similar identity security requirements, granting consumers greater control over their personal information. Organizations that collect, store, or process California residents' data must implement identity security measures to prevent unauthorized access, theft, or exposure of sensitive credentials. Under CCPA, consumers have the right to request access to their stored identity data, opt out of data sharing, and demand deletion of their personal information. Failure to comply with CCPA security requirements can result in significant legal penalties and lawsuits, particularly in cases of identity-related data breaches.

For organizations handling financial transactions, compliance with the Payment Card Industry Data Security Standard (PCI DSS) is essential. PCI DSS mandates robust identity authentication measures to prevent fraud and unauthorized access to payment card information. Organizations must enforce multi-factor authentication (MFA), regularly update access controls, and conduct periodic access reviews to ensure that only authorized personnel can access payment processing systems. Additionally, PCI DSS requires logging and monitoring of all identity-related access attempts to detect and mitigate potential identity compromises. Non-compliance with PCI DSS can result in fines, increased transaction fees, and potential revocation of the ability to process credit card payments.

In the healthcare sector, the Health Insurance Portability and Accountability Act (HIPAA) establishes strict identity security requirements for protecting patient records and electronic health information (ePHI). Healthcare providers, insurers, and business associates must implement strong IAM controls to prevent unauthorized access to medical records. HIPAA mandates access management policies, identity verification measures, and audit logging to track all access attempts. Organizations must also conduct regular risk assessments to evaluate identity security vulnerabilities. Failure to comply with HIPAA identity security regulations can result in substantial financial penalties and legal action, particularly in cases of patient identity theft or unauthorized access to medical records.

The Sarbanes-Oxley Act (SOX) imposes identity security requirements on publicly traded companies to ensure financial data integrity and prevent fraudulent activities. Organizations subject to SOX compliance must enforce strict access controls, monitor privileged user activity, and implement identity-based audit trails to track financial transactions. Identity security controls play a crucial role in preventing insider threats, fraudulent accounting practices, and unauthorized modifications to financial records. SOX compliance requires organizations to regularly review access permissions, conduct identity risk assessments, and implement security measures to protect sensitive financial data.

Identity security is also a critical component of compliance with the Federal Information Security Management Act (FISMA), which governs cybersecurity standards for federal agencies and contractors in the United States. FISMA mandates strict identity authentication, access control, and user activity monitoring for all federal information systems. Organizations must implement Identity and Access Management (IAM) solutions to verify user identities, enforce least privilege access, and continuously monitor authentication logs for suspicious activity. Non-compliance with FISMA can result in loss of government contracts and legal consequences.

The NIST Cybersecurity Framework, developed by the U.S. National Institute of Standards and Technology, provides identity security best practices for organizations across industries. The framework emphasizes identity governance, risk-based authentication, continuous monitoring, and incident response planning. While not legally binding, many regulatory frameworks and industry standards reference NIST guidelines as a benchmark for identity security compliance. Organizations that align their identity security strategies with NIST recommendations can improve compliance with multiple regulatory requirements.

As identity security regulations continue to evolve, organizations must implement compliance-driven IAM strategies that incorporate zero trust security principles. Zero Trust requires continuous identity verification, contextual authentication, and strict access control enforcement to minimize the risk of unauthorized access. Many regulatory bodies recommend Zero Trust as a best practice for identity security, particularly in cloud environments where traditional perimeter-based security models are insufficient.

To maintain compliance with identity security regulations, organizations should implement automated compliance monitoring and identity threat detection tools. Security Information and Event Management (SIEM) solutions, User and Entity Behavior Analytics (UEBA), and Privileged Access Management (PAM) platforms help detect identity threats, enforce access policies, and generate compliance reports. Automated compliance monitoring enables organizations to proactively identify security gaps, enforce regulatory requirements, and streamline audit processes.

In addition to technical controls, organizations must invest in employee training and security awareness programs to comply with identity security regulations. Many compliance frameworks, including GDPR, HIPAA, and PCI DSS, require organizations to educate employees on secure authentication practices, phishing awareness, and identity risk management. Security awareness training helps prevent identity-based attacks, reduces the risk of human error, and ensures that employees follow regulatory requirements when handling sensitive identity information.

Legal and compliance considerations for identity security extend beyond regulatory requirements to include contractual obligations with business partners, vendors, and third-party service providers. Many organizations require vendors to comply with strict identity security policies, including multi-factor authentication enforcement, role-based access control, and regular security assessments. Contracts and Service Level Agreements (SLAs) often specify identity security requirements to ensure that third-party access does not introduce compliance risks. Organizations must regularly assess vendor compliance with identity security policies to mitigate supply chain risks.

Given the increasing regulatory scrutiny on identity security, organizations must take a proactive approach to compliance by continuously assessing risks, updating policies, and adopting advanced IAM solutions. By aligning identity security practices with legal requirements, businesses can reduce regulatory risks, enhance data protection, and maintain trust with customers, partners, and stakeholders.

Red Teaming and Identity Security Testing

Red teaming is a proactive security approach that simulates real-world attacks to test an organization's ability to detect, respond to, and mitigate identity-related threats. Unlike traditional penetration testing, which focuses on finding vulnerabilities in specific systems, red teaming takes a broader perspective by emulating advanced threat actors attempting to compromise identities, escalate privileges, and move laterally within an organization. By conducting controlled adversarial simulations, organizations can evaluate the effectiveness of their identity security controls, improve their detection and response capabilities, and strengthen their overall cybersecurity posture.

Identity security testing in red teaming exercises involves assessing various aspects of authentication, authorization, and access management. Attackers frequently target weak authentication mechanisms, misconfigured identity and access management (IAM) policies, and overprivileged accounts to gain unauthorized access. Red teamers mimic these attack techniques to identify gaps in identity security defenses. By simulating credential theft, phishing attacks, and MFA bypass attempts, security teams can determine how well an organization can detect and prevent unauthorized access.

One of the primary objectives of red teaming in identity security is testing the resilience of authentication mechanisms. Many organizations rely on passwords as the primary form of authentication, but weak passwords, password reuse, and credential stuffing attacks pose significant risks. Red teamers use automated tools to conduct password spraying attacks, testing whether common or weak passwords are still in use. They also attempt brute-force attacks on systems that do not enforce account lockouts or rate-limiting protections. These tests help organizations identify weak authentication practices and implement stronger policies, such as enforcing multi-factor authentication (MFA) and passwordless authentication.

MFA bypass testing is another critical component of identity security red teaming. While MFA provides an additional layer of security, it is not immune to attacks. Red teamers attempt various techniques to bypass MFA, including social engineering attacks, real-time phishing proxies, and MFA fatigue attacks. In an MFA fatigue attack, attackers repeatedly send authentication requests to a user until they approve one out of frustration or confusion. By testing how employees and security systems respond to MFA bypass attempts, organizations can refine their authentication policies and enforce more resilient MFA methods, such as hardware security keys or biometric authentication.

Phishing simulations play a crucial role in red teaming identity security. Attackers commonly use phishing emails, text messages (smishing), and voice calls (vishing) to trick users into revealing their credentials. Red teamers craft realistic phishing campaigns that mimic real-world threats, targeting employees with fake login pages, urgent security notifications, or impersonated executive emails. These exercises measure how susceptible employees are to phishing attacks and help organizations improve their security awareness training programs. Advanced red teaming exercises also test the organization's ability to detect and respond to compromised accounts resulting from successful phishing attacks.

Once an initial foothold is established, red teamers test an organization's ability to detect and prevent privilege escalation. Attackers who gain access to a low-level user account often attempt to escalate privileges by exploiting misconfigured IAM policies, weak administrator credentials, or unmonitored service accounts. Red teamers analyze privilege inheritance, group memberships, and access control lists to identify potential privilege escalation paths. They also test whether role-based access control (RBAC) and attribute-based access control (ABAC) policies are properly enforced. These tests help organizations refine their access management policies and implement least privilege access controls.

Lateral movement testing is another essential aspect of identity security red teaming. After gaining elevated privileges, attackers often attempt to move laterally across systems to access more valuable assets, such as financial data, intellectual property, or critical infrastructure. Red teamers simulate these techniques by abusing identity federation, exploiting single sign-on (SSO) misconfigurations, or leveraging stolen authentication tokens. By testing how easily an attacker can pivot within the network, organizations can identify weaknesses in their identity segmentation strategies and implement stronger monitoring controls.

Red team exercises also assess the effectiveness of identity threat detection and response mechanisms. Many organizations use security information and event management (SIEM) solutions, user and entity behavior analytics (UEBA), and identity threat detection and response (ITDR) tools to monitor for anomalous identity activity. Red teamers test whether these tools can detect suspicious authentication attempts, privilege escalations, and unauthorized access. If security teams fail to detect red team activities, it indicates gaps in visibility and monitoring that need to be addressed. Organizations can then fine-tune their detection rules, improve log correlation, and enhance alert prioritization to strengthen their response capabilities.

Cloud identity security is another critical focus of red teaming exercises. Many organizations rely on cloud-based IAM solutions, such as Microsoft Azure Active Directory, Okta, or AWS Identity and Access Management (IAM). Red teamers attempt to exploit weak IAM policies, misconfigured API permissions, and excessive service account privileges in cloud environments. They also test whether security teams can detect unauthorized cloud authentication attempts, API abuse, and suspicious access patterns. By identifying weaknesses in cloud identity security, organizations can enforce stronger access policies, implement conditional access controls, and improve cloud security monitoring.

Red teaming also evaluates the effectiveness of incident response plans related to identity security. When a red team successfully compromises an identity, security teams must detect the breach, contain the threat, and remediate the affected accounts. Red teamers observe how quickly security teams identify and respond to the simulated attack, testing whether automated response mechanisms, such as disabling compromised accounts or revoking authentication tokens, function as intended. Organizations use the results of these exercises to refine their incident response playbooks, improve communication between teams, and implement automated remediation workflows.

Identity security testing through red teaming provides organizations with valuable insights into their strengths and weaknesses. By simulating real-world attacks, organizations can proactively identify and address identity vulnerabilities before they are exploited by malicious actors. Continuous red teaming exercises help organizations stay ahead of evolving threats, improve employee security awareness, and refine their identity security policies. The insights gained from these tests enable organizations to implement more robust identity security controls, ensuring better protection against credential theft, privilege abuse, and unauthorized access.

By integrating red teaming into their overall security strategy, organizations can build a more resilient identity security posture, enhance their ability to detect and respond to identity threats, and reduce the risk of identity-related breaches. Through continuous testing and refinement, organizations can improve their IAM policies, enforce stronger authentication mechanisms, and develop a proactive approach to identity security that keeps pace with emerging cyber threats.

Threat Modeling for Identity-Based Attacks

Threat modeling for identity-based attacks is a proactive security approach that helps organizations identify, assess, and mitigate risks related to user identities, authentication mechanisms, and access control systems. As cybercriminals increasingly target credentials, privilege escalation paths, and authentication weaknesses, organizations must develop structured threat models to understand potential attack vectors and design effective security countermeasures. By systematically analyzing how attackers might exploit identity vulnerabilities, organizations can strengthen their identity security posture and reduce the risk of unauthorized access, credential theft, and account compromise.

A comprehensive identity threat model begins with identifying the assets that require protection. In an identity security context, these assets include user credentials, authentication systems, privileged accounts, identity federation mechanisms, multi-factor authentication (MFA) tokens, and access control policies. Additionally, organizations must consider machine identities, such as API keys, service accounts, and cloud authentication tokens, as attackers frequently target these non-human credentials to infiltrate networks and escalate privileges. Understanding the assets at risk allows organizations to prioritize security controls and allocate resources effectively.

Once assets are identified, organizations must analyze potential attack surfaces that adversaries might exploit. Common attack surfaces in identity security include web login portals, single sign-on (SSO) systems, password reset mechanisms, identity provider (IdP) integrations, cloud IAM platforms, and remote access solutions. Attackers often exploit misconfigurations, weak authentication policies, and unmonitored privileged accounts to gain unauthorized access. Threat modeling helps security teams map out these attack surfaces and assess how an adversary could compromise them.

Attackers leverage various techniques to exploit identity-based weaknesses. One of the most common methods is credential theft, where cybercriminals use phishing attacks, malware, or brute-force attacks to obtain user passwords. Threat modeling evaluates how adversaries might gain access to credentials and what security controls can mitigate these risks. Organizations can enforce strong password policies, implement password managers, and deploy adaptive authentication mechanisms to counter credential theft. Additionally, the use of AI-powered security tools can help detect anomalous authentication patterns that may indicate stolen credentials.

Another critical attack vector in identity threat modeling is privilege escalation. Once attackers gain access to a low-privileged account, they often attempt to elevate their privileges to gain deeper access into an organization's infrastructure. Threat modeling helps identify potential privilege escalation paths, such as excessive permissions, misconfigured role assignments, and unprotected administrator accounts. Organizations can mitigate privilege escalation risks by enforcing least privilege access (LPA), implementing just-in-time (JIT) access controls, and continuously monitoring privilege changes within identity systems.

Lateral movement is another key concern in identity-based threat modeling. Attackers who compromise an identity often attempt to move across the network by abusing identity federation, exploiting weak session management, or leveraging compromised service accounts. Threat modeling evaluates how attackers might pivot within an environment and what security measures can prevent them from doing so. Organizations can implement network segmentation, enforce strict session timeouts, and monitor authentication logs to detect and prevent unauthorized lateral movement.

Multi-factor authentication (MFA) bypass techniques are also analyzed in identity threat modeling. While MFA provides an additional layer of security, attackers have developed sophisticated techniques to circumvent it. These include MFA fatigue attacks, SIM swapping, and man-in-the-middle (MITM) phishing attacks that intercept authentication tokens. Organizations can model potential MFA bypass scenarios and deploy phishing-resistant authentication methods, such as FIDO2 security keys or certificate-based authentication, to strengthen their defenses.

Identity federation and single sign-on (SSO) introduce additional security challenges that must be considered in threat modeling. While SSO improves user convenience and reduces password fatigue, it also creates a single point of failure if compromised. Attackers who gain access to an SSO session can access multiple applications without needing to authenticate again. Threat modeling helps security teams evaluate the risks associated with SSO and implement compensating controls, such as conditional access policies, continuous authentication, and risk-based session monitoring.

API security plays a crucial role in identity threat modeling, especially as organizations rely on cloud services and third-party integrations. Attackers often target API authentication mechanisms, exploiting weak API keys, misconfigured OAuth permissions, and insufficient API access controls. Organizations should model potential API attack scenarios and enforce strong API security practices, including token expiration policies, rate limiting, and API behavior monitoring. By integrating API security into identity threat models, organizations can reduce the risk of unauthorized access to cloud-based resources.

Account recovery mechanisms are another area that requires careful threat modeling. Many identity-based attacks involve exploiting weak password reset processes, such as using knowledge-based authentication (KBA) questions that can be easily guessed or socially engineered. Attackers also target email-based password reset links, intercepting them to take control of user accounts. Organizations can use threat modeling to evaluate weaknesses in account recovery processes and implement stronger recovery mechanisms, such as biometric authentication, hardware-backed security keys, and out-of-band verification.

Insider threats represent a unique identity security risk that must be incorporated into threat modeling. Malicious insiders, disgruntled employees, or compromised contractors may abuse their legitimate access to steal data, modify critical systems, or disable security controls. Threat modeling helps organizations identify potential insider threat scenarios and implement countermeasures such as continuous user behavior monitoring, privilege usage tracking, and automated identity risk scoring. By analyzing insider threat risks, organizations can enforce stricter access policies and detect anomalous behavior before it leads to security incidents.

Zero Trust security principles play a vital role in identity threat modeling, as they assume that no identity should be inherently trusted, regardless of its location or access level. A Zero Trust approach requires continuous authentication, real-time risk assessments, and micro-segmentation of identity access. Threat modeling can help organizations design Zero Trust architectures by identifying identity-based weaknesses and implementing policies that enforce strict access verification at every stage of authentication and authorization.

The effectiveness of identity threat modeling depends on continuous iteration and adaptation to emerging threats. Organizations should regularly update their threat models based on new attack techniques, evolving business requirements, and changes in IT infrastructure. Security teams should conduct red teaming exercises, penetration tests, and simulated attacks to validate the assumptions in their threat models and improve their security controls accordingly.

Threat modeling for identity-based attacks provides organizations with a structured approach to identifying security gaps, prioritizing mitigation strategies, and strengthening overall identity security. By analyzing potential attack vectors, evaluating security controls, and continuously refining their identity security posture, organizations can effectively defend against modern identity threats and reduce the risk of unauthorized access, data breaches, and credential abuse.

Deception Techniques in Identity Security

Deception techniques in identity security have gained significant attention as organizations strive to outmaneuver increasingly sophisticated cyber threats. These techniques involve misleading attackers by deploying decoys, traps, and false information to disrupt their reconnaissance and exploitation efforts. Unlike traditional security measures that focus on preventing unauthorized access, deception-based strategies aim to misdirect, confuse, and expose malicious actors before they can inflict damage. By leveraging deception, organizations can gain valuable intelligence on attack patterns, reduce dwell time, and enhance their overall security posture.

One of the core principles of deception in identity security is the strategic placement of decoy credentials, accounts, and systems. These decoys appear legitimate to attackers, enticing them into revealing their methods and intentions. For instance, organizations may create fake user accounts with seemingly valuable access privileges, luring cybercriminals into interacting with them. Once an attacker engages with these deceptive assets, security teams can track their movements, analyze their techniques, and respond proactively. This approach not only increases the chances of detecting unauthorized access but also minimizes the risk of real identity compromise.

Another powerful deception method involves the use of honeypots and honeytokens. Honeypots are specially designed systems that mimic real IT infrastructure but have no actual business function. When an attacker attempts to exploit a honeypot, security teams receive an immediate alert, allowing them to study the attack in a controlled environment. Similarly, honeytokens are pieces of data—such as fake API keys, credentials, or files—that serve as bait. If an adversary accesses or attempts to use a honeytoken, security teams can trace the intrusion back to its source. These techniques provide valuable insights into emerging threats and enable organizations to refine their security defenses accordingly.

A key aspect of deception in identity security is the creation of false attack surfaces. By manipulating the perceived structure of an organization's identity landscape, security teams can lead attackers down misleading paths. This may include the deployment of fake directory structures, misleading access control policies, or simulated user behavior. For example, an organization might configure a set of seemingly privileged accounts with no actual access rights but with detailed logging enabled. If an attacker attempts to compromise these accounts, security teams gain crucial intelligence about their tactics. This proactive approach allows defenders to anticipate and neutralize threats before they escalate.

In addition to luring attackers with fake assets, deception techniques can also be used to disrupt their operations. Misinformation campaigns within an organization's digital environment can introduce uncertainty and doubt into an attacker's decision-making process. By dynamically altering credentials, changing file structures, or injecting misleading logs, defenders can create an unpredictable environment that forces adversaries to expend more time and resources. This strategy increases the likelihood that an attack will be detected before it reaches a critical stage.

Machine learning and artificial intelligence play an increasingly important role in deception-based security strategies. Automated deception platforms can generate realistic but fake identities, credentials, and user activity patterns to confuse attackers. These platforms analyze attack behavior in real time and adapt their deception tactics accordingly. For instance, if an attacker is probing for high-value accounts, the system can dynamically generate and present deceptive accounts that appear increasingly valuable as the adversary continues their attack. This adaptive approach makes deception strategies more effective and scalable.

The psychological impact of deception on attackers is another critical factor in its effectiveness. Cybercriminals rely on predictability and logical patterns to execute their attacks efficiently. When they encounter deceptive elements, their confidence in their understanding of the target environment is shaken. This can lead to hesitation, mistakes, or even abandonment of the attack. In some cases, attackers may inadvertently reveal additional information about their methods as they attempt to navigate the deceptive environment. By leveraging psychological tactics, deception techniques create an additional layer of defense that goes beyond technical security controls.

Despite its advantages, deception in identity security must be carefully implemented to avoid unintended consequences. Poorly designed deception tactics can introduce unnecessary complexity, create operational inefficiencies, or even mislead legitimate users. For deception to be effective, it must seamlessly integrate with an organization's broader security framework. Security teams must continuously monitor and refine their deceptive assets to ensure they remain convincing and effective against evolving threats. Additionally, legal and ethical considerations must be taken into account, especially when dealing with attackers who may be located in different jurisdictions.

Organizations that adopt deception techniques as part of their identity security strategy can significantly enhance their ability to detect, deter, and respond to cyber threats. By misleading attackers and turning their reconnaissance efforts against them, deception provides a proactive and intelligence-driven approach to cybersecurity. As cyber threats continue to evolve, deception-based strategies will play an increasingly vital role in protecting sensitive identity data and ensuring the integrity of organizational security.

Threats to Identity Federation and SSO

Identity federation and single sign-on (SSO) have become essential components of modern authentication frameworks, allowing users to access multiple applications with a single set of credentials. These technologies enhance user experience, reduce password fatigue, and improve security by minimizing the need for multiple credentials. However, they also introduce significant security risks that attackers can exploit. Threats to identity federation and SSO range from credential theft to protocol vulnerabilities, and organizations must implement robust security measures to mitigate these risks.

One of the most prominent threats to identity federation and SSO is credential compromise. Since SSO allows users to access multiple services with a single authentication event, a successful credential theft can grant attackers access to a vast number of systems. Phishing attacks remain one of the most common methods for stealing credentials. Cybercriminals create fake login pages that mimic legitimate identity providers, tricking users into entering their credentials. Once the attacker obtains these credentials, they can impersonate the victim across all federated services, leading to potential data breaches and account takeovers.

Man-in-the-middle (MITM) attacks pose another significant risk to identity federation and SSO. Attackers can intercept authentication requests and steal authentication tokens by exploiting weaknesses in communication channels. If an attacker successfully captures a session token, they can replay it to gain unauthorized access. Without strong encryption and proper session handling, federated authentication flows become vulnerable to interception. Organizations that fail to secure their authentication mechanisms with measures such as mutual TLS, signed assertions, and token expiration controls expose themselves to these types of attacks.

Session hijacking is another concern in federated authentication environments. Attackers who gain access to a user's session can bypass authentication mechanisms altogether. This can happen through various techniques, including session fixation, where an attacker forces a user to authenticate using a pre-defined session ID. Once authentication is completed, the attacker assumes control of the session without needing to steal the actual credentials. Similarly, cross-site scripting (XSS) attacks can be leveraged to extract session tokens from a user's browser and use them to gain unauthorized access to federated resources.

Protocol weaknesses in identity federation frameworks also present serious security risks. Standards such as Security Assertion Markup Language (SAML), OpenID Connect (OIDC), and OAuth 2.0 define the mechanisms for identity federation, but improper implementations can lead to vulnerabilities. For example, XML signature wrapping attacks in SAML can allow attackers to modify authentication assertions without breaking their cryptographic integrity. Similarly, poorly validated redirect URIs in OAuth can enable open redirect attacks, where users are tricked into authorizing malicious applications. If identity providers do not rigorously validate authentication requests and responses, attackers can exploit protocol flaws to bypass authentication.

Token theft and misuse are additional threats that can compromise federated authentication. Identity federation relies on tokens to establish trust between identity providers and service providers. If an attacker steals an access token, they can use it to gain unauthorized access to resources without needing to authenticate again. Token leakage can occur through insecure storage, browser-based vulnerabilities, or API exposure. In cases where refresh tokens are compromised, attackers may maintain persistent access by continuously obtaining new access tokens. Implementing proper token security mechanisms, such as short-lived tokens, audience restrictions, and token binding, is crucial to mitigating these risks.

Insider threats also play a role in the security challenges of identity federation and SSO. Employees or privileged users with access to authentication infrastructure can exploit their positions to manipulate authentication flows or extract sensitive credentials. A malicious administrator could configure a rogue identity provider or modify authentication policies to allow unauthorized access. Even unintentional misconfigurations by well-meaning employees can expose identity federation to attacks. Organizations must enforce strict access controls, implement least privilege principles, and monitor authentication activity to detect and prevent insider threats.

Social engineering attacks further exacerbate the risks associated with identity federation. Attackers use psychological manipulation to trick users or administrators into revealing authentication secrets. They may impersonate IT support staff, sending emails or making phone calls to convince users to provide access credentials. Business Email Compromise (BEC) schemes have also been used to exploit federated authentication, where attackers hijack legitimate email accounts and use them to request password resets or SSO access approvals. Educating users about social engineering tactics and implementing multi-factor authentication (MFA) can help mitigate these types of attacks.

Availability threats are another critical concern for federated identity systems. If an identity provider experiences downtime or a denial-of-service (DoS) attack, users may be unable to authenticate and access services. This can disrupt business operations and create security blind spots. Attackers may exploit this by launching DoS attacks against identity providers, preventing legitimate users from logging in while they attempt credential stuffing or brute-force attacks. Redundant authentication infrastructure, rate limiting, and anomaly detection can help mitigate the risk of authentication service disruptions.

Misconfigured access policies in identity federation frameworks can lead to privilege escalation and unauthorized access. If role-based access controls (RBAC) and attribute-based access controls (ABAC) are not properly configured, users may inherit permissions beyond what they should have. This can be exploited by attackers who gain access to a low-privileged account and escalate their privileges within a federated system. Organizations must implement strict access control policies, continuously review permissions, and enforce the principle of least privilege to reduce the risk of privilege escalation.

While identity federation and SSO offer significant benefits in terms of usability and security, they introduce complex attack surfaces that require careful protection. Organizations must implement strong authentication mechanisms, continuously monitor authentication activity, and address vulnerabilities in federation protocols to minimize risks. By proactively securing federated authentication systems, organizations can enhance their identity security posture and reduce the likelihood of breaches.

Cloud Access Security Brokers and Identity Protection

As organizations increasingly migrate to cloud environments, securing access to cloud-based resources has become a top priority. Traditional security perimeters have dissolved, leaving identity as the primary security boundary. Cloud Access Security Brokers (CASBs) play a crucial role in addressing this challenge by acting as intermediaries between users and cloud services. CASBs provide visibility, enforce security policies, and enhance identity protection by monitoring and controlling access to cloud applications. Their ability to integrate with identity and access management (IAM) solutions makes them essential in safeguarding enterprise data in a cloud-first world.

One of the key functions of CASBs is visibility into cloud usage. Shadow IT—the use of unsanctioned cloud applications—poses a significant risk to organizations. Employees often adopt cloud services without IT approval, exposing sensitive data to potential breaches. CASBs help detect and monitor the use of unauthorized applications by analyzing network traffic and authentication logs. By providing comprehensive insights into cloud usage patterns, CASBs enable organizations to assess risks, enforce compliance, and prevent data exfiltration. Without this visibility, security teams lack the necessary context to protect cloud-based assets effectively.

CASBs also play a critical role in enforcing security policies across cloud environments. Organizations often struggle with inconsistent security configurations across different cloud providers and applications. CASBs standardize security controls, ensuring that access policies align with corporate security requirements. They enforce authentication mechanisms, data encryption policies, and access restrictions based on contextual factors such as user location, device type, and risk level. By integrating with identity providers and single sign-on (SSO) solutions, CASBs enhance authentication security and reduce the risk of unauthorized access.

One of the most valuable aspects of CASBs is their ability to prevent data loss. Cloud services store vast amounts of sensitive information, including intellectual property, financial records, and personally identifiable information (PII). If improperly managed, these data assets can be exposed to external threats or internal misuse. CASBs implement data loss prevention (DLP) policies that automatically detect and block unauthorized data transfers. They classify and monitor sensitive information, applying encryption, redaction, or access restrictions as needed. By preventing data leakage, CASBs help organizations maintain regulatory compliance and protect customer trust.

CASBs also enhance identity protection through advanced threat detection mechanisms. Cybercriminals frequently target cloud-based identities using tactics such as phishing, brute-force attacks, and credential stuffing. CASBs analyze authentication behaviors, detecting anomalies that may indicate compromised accounts. By leveraging machine learning, CASBs can identify suspicious login attempts, impossible travel scenarios, and unusual access patterns. When a threat is detected, CASBs can enforce step-up authentication, requiring additional verification before granting access. This proactive approach significantly reduces the risk of unauthorized access and identity-based attacks.

Integration with multi-factor authentication (MFA) further strengthens identity security within CASB deployments. Many cloud applications still rely on weak password-based authentication, making them susceptible to credential theft. CASBs enable organizations to enforce MFA policies across all cloud services, ensuring that users verify their identities through additional authentication factors such as biometrics, security keys, or mobile authentication apps. By requiring MFA for high-risk transactions or privileged access requests, CASBs minimize the likelihood of account compromise, even if credentials are stolen.

Another critical function of CASBs is managing privileged access in cloud environments. Administrative accounts and privileged users have extensive access rights, making them prime targets for attackers. If compromised, these accounts can be used to manipulate cloud configurations, steal data, or disrupt business operations. CASBs enforce just-in-time access controls, ensuring that users receive elevated privileges only when necessary and for a limited duration. By monitoring privileged activity and implementing least-privilege access principles, CASBs help prevent insider threats and reduce the attack surface.

CASBs also play a role in mitigating risks associated with third-party integrations. Many organizations connect cloud applications with third-party services, such as SaaS platforms, APIs, and external vendors. These integrations often require access to sensitive data, increasing the risk of supply chain attacks. CASBs assess the security posture of third-party applications, enforcing policies that restrict access to only trusted services. They provide detailed audit logs of third-party interactions, enabling organizations to monitor and review access permissions. By controlling third-party access, CASBs prevent unauthorized data sharing and reduce supply chain vulnerabilities.

Compliance enforcement is another major benefit of CASBs, especially for organizations operating in regulated industries. Cloud providers offer varying levels of security, and ensuring compliance with data protection laws such as GDPR, HIPAA, and PCI-DSS can be challenging. CASBs streamline compliance efforts by continuously monitoring cloud activities, generating audit trails, and enforcing industry-specific security standards. Automated policy enforcement ensures that sensitive data is stored, processed, and shared in accordance with regulatory requirements. By simplifying compliance management, CASBs help organizations avoid costly penalties and legal repercussions.

As cyber threats continue to evolve, CASBs are incorporating artificial intelligence (AI) and automation to enhance security capabilities. AI-driven CASBs analyze vast amounts of cloud activity data, identifying trends and predicting potential security incidents. Automated response mechanisms allow CASBs to take immediate action against threats, such as revoking access tokens, isolating compromised accounts, or blocking high-risk transactions. This adaptive security model ensures that organizations can respond to threats in real time, minimizing the impact of cloud-based attacks.

By acting as a security control point between users and cloud applications, CASBs provide a multi-layered defense against identity threats. Their ability to enforce authentication policies, prevent data loss, and detect anomalous behavior makes them indispensable for organizations with a strong cloud presence. As cloud adoption continues to grow, the role of CASBs in identity protection will become increasingly vital, ensuring that organizations can maintain security, compliance, and control in an ever-expanding digital landscape.

Biometric Authentication: Benefits and Challenges

Biometric authentication has emerged as a powerful security mechanism, leveraging unique physical or behavioral traits to verify identity. Unlike traditional authentication methods that rely on passwords or PINs, biometrics provide a seamless and secure way to access systems and services. From fingerprint and facial recognition to voice and iris scanning, biometric authentication offers a more user-friendly and robust approach to identity verification. However, while the technology brings numerous benefits, it also presents significant challenges related to privacy, security, and implementation.

One of the key advantages of biometric authentication is its convenience. Users no longer need to remember complex passwords or worry about forgetting login credentials. A simple fingerprint scan or facial recognition process allows for quick and frictionless access to devices, applications, and secure environments. This ease of use has made biometrics particularly popular in consumer technology, with smartphones, laptops, and banking apps integrating fingerprint and facial recognition to enhance user experience. The reduction in reliance on passwords also mitigates issues like password fatigue and poor password management practices, which are common vulnerabilities in traditional authentication systems.

Security is another major benefit of biometric authentication. Since biometric traits are unique to individuals, they provide a higher level of assurance compared to knowledge-based authentication methods. Passwords and PINs can be guessed, stolen, or shared, whereas biometric data is inherently tied to the individual. This uniqueness makes biometric authentication more resistant to brute-force attacks and credential theft. Additionally, many biometric systems use advanced encryption and liveness detection to prevent spoofing attempts, further strengthening security. When implemented correctly, biometrics significantly reduce the risk of unauthorized access and identity fraud.

Another advantage of biometric authentication is its potential to improve access control in high-security environments. Organizations handling sensitive data, such as financial institutions, government agencies, and healthcare providers, benefit from the added layer of security that biometrics provide. Multi-factor authentication (MFA) often incorporates biometrics alongside other factors, such as smart cards or PINs, to create a more secure authentication framework. This approach enhances identity verification while maintaining usability, making biometrics a preferred choice for securing critical infrastructure and confidential information.

Despite its advantages, biometric authentication also faces several challenges. One of the primary concerns is privacy. Unlike passwords, biometric data is immutable—once compromised, it cannot be changed. If an attacker steals a password, the user can reset it. However, if biometric data is leaked or misused, there is no way to replace a fingerprint or iris pattern. This creates long-term security risks, particularly if biometric databases are breached. Unauthorized collection and storage of biometric information also raise ethical and regulatory concerns, as individuals may have limited control over how their data is used.

The risk of biometric spoofing and presentation attacks is another challenge in biometric authentication. Cybercriminals have developed sophisticated techniques to replicate biometric traits using 3D-printed fingerprints, high-resolution facial images, and synthetic voice recordings. Although liveness detection and anti-spoofing technologies help mitigate these threats, determined attackers can still find ways to bypass biometric systems. In cases where biometric authentication is the sole security measure, successful spoofing can result in significant security breaches. To address this risk, many organizations combine biometrics with additional authentication factors to create a more resilient security model.

Another issue with biometric authentication is its susceptibility to false positives and false negatives. No biometric system is perfect, and errors in recognition can impact both security and usability. False positives occur when an unauthorized person is mistakenly granted access, while false negatives prevent legitimate users from authenticating successfully. Factors such as poor sensor quality, environmental conditions, and changes in biometric traits due to aging or injuries can affect accuracy. Organizations must carefully calibrate their biometric systems to strike a balance between security and user accessibility, ensuring that authentication remains both reliable and efficient.

Scalability and integration challenges also pose obstacles to widespread biometric adoption. Deploying biometric authentication across large organizations or public services requires significant infrastructure investment. Biometric scanners, storage solutions, and processing capabilities must be integrated seamlessly with existing identity management systems. Additionally, interoperability between different biometric platforms and standards remains a challenge. A lack of universal standards can lead to compatibility issues, making it difficult for organizations to implement a consistent biometric authentication framework across multiple systems and devices.

Regulatory and legal considerations further complicate biometric authentication. Many countries have enacted strict data protection laws, such as the General Data Protection Regulation (GDPR) in Europe, which impose stringent requirements on the collection, storage, and processing of biometric data. Organizations must ensure compliance with these regulations to avoid legal repercussions. Ethical concerns regarding biometric surveillance and mass data collection have also sparked debates about the potential misuse of biometric technology by governments and corporations. As biometric authentication becomes more prevalent, striking a balance between security, privacy, and regulatory compliance will be essential.

The advancement of artificial intelligence (AI) and machine learning (ML) has introduced new opportunities and challenges in biometric authentication. AI-powered biometric systems can enhance accuracy and adaptability by continuously learning from user interactions. However, these systems also raise concerns about bias and discrimination. Studies have shown that some biometric technologies, particularly facial recognition, exhibit racial and gender-based biases, leading to higher error rates for certain demographics. Addressing these biases requires ongoing research, diverse training datasets, and transparent algorithmic development to ensure fairness and inclusivity in biometric authentication systems.

While biometric authentication offers undeniable benefits in terms of security, convenience, and user experience, its adoption must be approached with caution. Organizations must implement strong encryption, data minimization strategies, and user consent mechanisms to protect biometric information. Combining biometrics with other authentication methods, such as device-based security and behavioral analytics, can further enhance identity protection. As technology evolves, biometric authentication will continue to play a crucial role in securing digital identities, but it must be deployed responsibly to mitigate risks and safeguard user privacy.

Identity Threats in Remote Work Environments

The widespread adoption of remote work has reshaped the cybersecurity landscape, introducing new identity threats that organizations must address. As employees access corporate resources from diverse locations and devices, traditional security perimeters have become obsolete. Identity has become the primary security control, but remote work environments create vulnerabilities that cybercriminals actively exploit. Weak authentication, unsecured networks, phishing attacks, and insider threats all contribute to the growing risk of identity compromise in remote work settings. Organizations must recognize these threats and implement comprehensive security strategies to protect their remote workforce.

One of the most significant identity threats in remote work environments is credential theft. Remote employees frequently log into corporate systems using personal devices and unsecured networks, making them prime targets for cybercriminals. Phishing attacks remain the most common method for stealing credentials. Attackers craft convincing emails, messages, or fake login portals that trick users into providing their credentials. Once stolen, these credentials can be used to access sensitive company data or sold on the dark web. Credential stuffing attacks, where attackers use leaked username-password combinations from previous breaches, further exacerbate this threat. Since employees often reuse passwords across multiple accounts, a single compromised credential can lead to widespread security breaches.

The use of weak authentication mechanisms also heightens the risk of identity compromise in remote work settings. Many employees rely solely on passwords, which are often easy to guess or crack. Without additional layers of authentication, such as multi-factor authentication (MFA), attackers can easily gain unauthorized access. MFA significantly reduces this risk by requiring an additional verification factor, such as a mobile authentication app, a security key, or a biometric scan. However, some organizations fail to enforce MFA across all remote access points, leaving gaps that attackers can exploit. Even when MFA is implemented, attackers use social engineering tactics to trick users into approving fraudulent login attempts, bypassing security controls.

Remote work environments also introduce risks associated with insecure networks. Unlike office settings, where security teams can control network access and enforce firewall protections, remote workers often connect to corporate systems from home networks, public Wi-Fi, or other untrusted environments. Home routers may have weak security configurations, outdated firmware, or default passwords that attackers can exploit. Public Wi-Fi networks, such as those in coffee shops or coworking spaces, pose even greater risks. Attackers can intercept traffic using man-in-the-middle (MITM) attacks, capturing login credentials and session tokens. Without the use of virtual private networks (VPNs) or secure web gateways, remote workers are vulnerable to network-based identity threats.

Another major identity risk in remote work environments is session hijacking. Many cloud-based applications and remote desktop solutions use session tokens to maintain user authentication across multiple interactions. If an attacker intercepts or steals a valid session token, they can impersonate the user without needing their password. This threat is particularly concerning when employees use shared or unsecured devices for work. A compromised session can grant attackers prolonged access to corporate resources, allowing them to exfiltrate data or launch additional attacks. Organizations must implement strict session expiration policies, token binding mechanisms, and endpoint security controls to mitigate this risk.

Insider threats pose additional identity risks in remote work settings. Employees working from home have greater autonomy over their devices and access privileges, making it more difficult for security teams to monitor unauthorized activities. Disgruntled employees or those facing financial difficulties may be tempted to misuse their access privileges to steal or sell company data. Additionally, unintentional insider threats occur when employees unknowingly expose sensitive information through misconfigurations, accidental sharing, or failing to follow security best practices. Without proper monitoring and access controls, insider threats can go undetected for extended periods, leading to severe security incidents.

The growing reliance on third-party collaboration tools and cloud services further complicates identity security in remote work environments. Employees frequently use applications such as file-sharing platforms, messaging services, and video conferencing tools to communicate and collaborate. If these applications are not properly secured, they can become entry points for attackers. Poorly configured access permissions, overprivileged user roles, and weak authentication measures in third-party services increase the risk of identity-related breaches. Attackers often exploit OAuth tokens, API keys, or Single Sign-On (SSO) misconfigurations to gain unauthorized access to corporate systems through compromised third-party applications.

Shadow IT also contributes to identity threats in remote work environments. Employees often use unsanctioned applications and services to improve productivity, but these tools may lack enterprise-grade security controls. Without IT oversight, unauthorized applications can introduce vulnerabilities, making it easier for attackers to compromise identities. Security teams may be unaware of these tools, leaving them unmonitored and susceptible to data leaks or credential theft. Organizations must implement cloud access security brokers (CASBs) and endpoint detection solutions to monitor and control the use of unauthorized applications.

Social engineering attacks continue to be a major concern for remote workers. Attackers exploit the isolation of remote employees, using tactics such as business email compromise (BEC), voice phishing (vishing), and SMS phishing (smishing) to gain access to sensitive information. Remote workers may be more susceptible to these attacks due to the lack of in-person verification and immediate support from IT teams. Attackers impersonate executives, IT staff, or trusted colleagues to manipulate employees into revealing credentials, approving fraudulent transactions, or granting remote access. Training and awareness programs are essential in equipping remote employees with the knowledge to recognize and resist social engineering attempts.

The lack of centralized monitoring and logging in remote work environments presents another challenge in identity security. Security teams struggle to track authentication attempts, access patterns, and potential anomalies across a distributed workforce. Without real-time visibility, detecting and responding to identity-related threats becomes more difficult. Implementing identity threat detection and response (ITDR) solutions helps organizations identify suspicious login attempts, privilege escalations, and unauthorized access to sensitive resources. AI-powered analytics can detect anomalies in user behavior, alerting security teams to potential identity compromises before they escalate.

The shift to remote work has fundamentally changed how organizations manage identity security. With traditional security perimeters no longer applicable, identity has become the focal point of enterprise security strategies. Organizations must adopt a multi-layered approach that includes strong authentication, network security measures, continuous monitoring, and user awareness training. By addressing the identity threats inherent in remote work environments, organizations can reduce the risk of breaches and ensure that remote employees can work securely without compromising sensitive data.

SIEM vs. XDR for Identity Security

As cyber threats targeting identity security become more sophisticated, organizations must adopt advanced security solutions to detect and respond to identity-based attacks. Security Information and Event Management (SIEM) and Extended Detection and Response (XDR) are two powerful tools that play crucial roles in identity security. While both solutions focus on detecting threats and responding to security incidents, they have distinct approaches, capabilities, and effectiveness in protecting identities. Understanding the differences between SIEM and XDR is essential for organizations looking to enhance their identity security posture.

SIEM has long been a foundational security technology for enterprises, providing centralized logging, correlation, and analysis of security events across an organization's IT infrastructure. SIEM solutions aggregate log data from various sources, including authentication systems, network devices, applications, and cloud environments. By applying correlation rules and analytics, SIEM platforms identify suspicious activities that may indicate compromised identities, such as failed login attempts, privilege escalations, or unusual access patterns. Security teams use SIEM to monitor authentication events, investigate incidents, and generate compliance reports.

A key advantage of SIEM in identity security is its ability to integrate with a wide range of identity-related data sources. Organizations can ingest logs from identity providers, single sign-on (SSO) solutions, multi-factor authentication (MFA) services, and privileged access management (PAM) systems. This provides a comprehensive view of authentication activities across the enterprise, helping security teams detect unauthorized access attempts, account takeovers, and insider threats. Additionally, SIEM platforms support compliance requirements by generating audit trails and maintaining historical authentication records for forensic analysis.

However, SIEM has limitations when it comes to real-time identity threat detection and response. Traditional SIEM platforms rely heavily on predefined rules and static correlation logic, which may struggle to detect sophisticated attacks that evolve over time. Attackers often use tactics such as credential stuffing, session hijacking, and lateral movement, which can bypass rule-based detection. SIEM solutions also generate a high volume of alerts, many of which are false positives, leading to alert fatigue for security teams. The manual effort required to investigate and respond to identity-related alerts can slow down response times, increasing the risk of breaches.

XDR, on the other hand, takes a more proactive and integrated approach to identity security. Unlike SIEM, which primarily focuses on log aggregation and correlation, XDR extends threat detection and response across multiple security layers, including endpoints, networks, email, cloud environments, and identity systems. By leveraging artificial intelligence (AI) and behavioral analytics, XDR detects identity-based threats in real time, providing a more automated and efficient response mechanism.

One of the primary strengths of XDR in identity security is its ability to correlate identity-related events with broader security telemetry. XDR platforms continuously analyze user behavior, detecting anomalies such as logins from unusual locations, impossible travel scenarios, and abnormal privilege escalations. By integrating identity security with endpoint and network security data, XDR can identify identity compromises that might go undetected by SIEM alone. For example, if an attacker gains access to an account and begins executing malicious activities on an endpoint, XDR can correlate the login event with suspicious process executions, enabling faster threat detection and containment.

Another advantage of XDR is its automated response capabilities. While SIEM primarily focuses on alerting security teams, XDR can take direct action to mitigate identity threats. When an anomalous authentication event is detected, XDR can automatically trigger security controls such as revoking access tokens, enforcing step-up authentication, or isolating compromised accounts. This reduces the time required to contain threats and minimizes the impact of identity-related security incidents. By integrating with identity and access management (IAM) solutions, XDR enhances identity security by enforcing adaptive authentication policies and continuous identity monitoring.

Despite its advanced capabilities, XDR is not a direct replacement for SIEM. SIEM excels at long-term data retention, compliance reporting, and forensic investigations, making it an essential component of enterprise security operations. XDR, while highly effective at detecting and responding to identity threats, may not provide the same depth of historical log analysis as SIEM. Organizations that require extensive compliance reporting and audit trails often rely on SIEM to meet regulatory requirements.

The decision between SIEM and XDR for identity security depends on an organization's security needs, resources, and threat landscape. Large enterprises with complex IT environments and regulatory requirements often use SIEM for centralized log management and compliance. However, to enhance identity threat detection and response, many organizations are adopting XDR as a complementary solution. By integrating XDR with SIEM, security teams can leverage the strengths of both technologies, combining SIEM's broad visibility with XDR's real-time threat detection and automated response capabilities.

As cyber threats targeting identity security continue to evolve, organizations must adopt a multi-layered approach to identity protection. SIEM provides the foundation for log aggregation and compliance, while XDR enhances threat detection and response by correlating identity signals with other security data. By leveraging both solutions effectively, organizations can strengthen their identity security posture, detect identity compromises faster, and minimize the risk of account takeovers and unauthorized access.

SOC Operations for Identity Threat Detection

Security Operations Centers (SOCs) play a crucial role in detecting and mitigating identity-related threats. As cybercriminals increasingly target user credentials, privilege escalation, and identity fraud, SOC teams must implement effective strategies to monitor and respond to identity-based attacks. Traditional security perimeters are no longer sufficient, making identity security a key focus for SOC operations. By leveraging advanced analytics, automation, and threat intelligence, SOCs can enhance their ability to detect and respond to identity threats in real time.

One of the primary responsibilities of a SOC in identity threat detection is monitoring authentication events. Attackers frequently attempt to compromise user accounts through brute-force attacks, credential stuffing, or phishing. SOC analysts continuously analyze login attempts, failed authentication events, and suspicious access patterns to identify potential identity compromises. For example, a sudden spike in failed login attempts from different IP addresses may indicate a credential stuffing attack. Similarly, logins from geographically distant locations within a short time frame suggest an impossible travel scenario, which could be a sign of account takeover.

Identity threat detection in SOC operations relies heavily on Security Information and Event Management (SIEM) platforms. SIEM solutions aggregate and correlate authentication logs from identity providers, single sign-on (SSO) systems, and multi-factor authentication (MFA) services. By applying correlation rules, SOC teams can identify anomalous behavior that deviates from normal user activity. For instance, if an employee who typically works from one geographic region suddenly logs in from multiple countries in a single day, the SIEM system can trigger an alert for further investigation. SOC analysts then assess whether the event is legitimate or part of an ongoing attack.

Extended Detection and Response (XDR) solutions further enhance identity threat detection by integrating identity telemetry with endpoint, network, and cloud security data. Unlike SIEM, which relies primarily on log analysis, XDR provides deeper visibility into identity threats by correlating user behavior with security events across the entire IT ecosystem. If a compromised account is used to access sensitive files and simultaneously triggers malware execution on an endpoint, XDR can identify the connection between the two events. This allows SOC analysts to respond to identity threats more effectively by understanding their broader impact.

Automation and orchestration are essential components of modern SOC operations for identity security. Manual analysis of identity threats can be time-consuming, leading to delayed response times. By leveraging Security Orchestration, Automation, and Response (SOAR) platforms, SOC teams can automate key processes such as user verification, account isolation, and incident triage. When an identity threat is detected, SOAR can automatically revoke access tokens, reset compromised passwords, or enforce step-up authentication for high-risk accounts. This reduces the window of opportunity for attackers and limits the damage caused by compromised credentials.

Threat intelligence also plays a critical role in SOC operations for identity security. Cybercriminals frequently use stolen credentials obtained from data breaches, phishing campaigns, or dark web marketplaces. SOC teams integrate threat intelligence feeds with their security platforms to detect the use of compromised credentials. If an employee's password appears in a known breach, SOC analysts can proactively enforce a password reset and monitor the account for suspicious activity. By staying ahead of emerging threats, SOC teams improve their ability to prevent identity compromises before they escalate.

Insider threats present additional challenges for SOC teams in identity threat detection. Unlike external attackers, malicious insiders already have access to corporate systems, making their activities harder to distinguish from legitimate behavior. SOC analysts use User and Entity Behavior Analytics (UEBA) to detect deviations from normal user activity that may indicate insider threats. If an employee suddenly accesses files outside their normal scope of work or attempts to escalate privileges, UEBA alerts SOC teams to potential risks. Continuous monitoring and access control policies help mitigate insider threats while ensuring that legitimate users are not falsely flagged.

Cloud environments introduce new identity security challenges that SOC teams must address. As organizations adopt cloud-based applications and infrastructure, identity becomes the primary security perimeter. SOC analysts monitor identity-related events in cloud platforms such as AWS, Microsoft Azure, and Google Cloud to detect unauthorized access attempts. Misconfigured access controls, overly permissive IAM roles, and compromised API keys can expose cloud environments to identity-based attacks. By enforcing least privilege access and continuously auditing cloud identities, SOC teams strengthen identity security in cloud-based ecosystems.

Multi-factor authentication (MFA) is a critical defense against identity threats, but attackers have developed techniques to bypass it. SOC teams monitor MFA bypass attempts, including SIM swapping attacks, push notification fatigue, and adversary-in-the-middle (AiTM) phishing. Attackers trick users into approving fraudulent authentication requests, granting them access to sensitive systems.

SOC analysts use adaptive authentication policies to require additional verification steps for high-risk logins, reducing the likelihood of successful MFA bypass attacks.

Incident response is a key function of SOC operations in identity security. When an identity compromise is detected, SOC teams follow predefined incident response procedures to contain the threat. This includes identifying the source of the compromise, revoking compromised credentials, and analyzing the attack vector to prevent future incidents. Digital forensics plays a crucial role in understanding how attackers gained access, allowing security teams to strengthen defenses. SOC teams also collaborate with IT and legal teams to ensure compliance with data protection regulations when responding to identity-related security incidents.

Security awareness training is an essential component of SOC operations for identity threat detection. Employees remain a significant target for phishing and social engineering attacks that aim to steal credentials. SOC teams work closely with security awareness programs to educate employees about identity threats, safe authentication practices, and recognizing phishing attempts. By fostering a security-conscious culture, organizations reduce the risk of identity-based attacks and enhance overall cybersecurity resilience.

As cyber threats targeting identities become more sophisticated, SOC teams must continuously evolve their strategies for identity threat detection. By integrating SIEM, XDR, SOAR, and threat intelligence, SOC operations enhance their ability to detect, investigate, and respond to identity-related threats. Automation, behavioral analytics, and continuous monitoring further strengthen identity security, ensuring that organizations remain protected against account takeovers, privilege escalations, and insider threats. Effective SOC operations not only detect identity threats in real time but also implement proactive measures to reduce risk and improve overall security posture.

Lessons from Real-World Identity Breaches

Identity breaches have become some of the most damaging cybersecurity incidents in recent years, exposing sensitive data, compromising critical infrastructure, and eroding public trust. Organizations of all sizes have suffered breaches due to poor identity security practices, inadequate authentication controls, and sophisticated cyberattacks. By analyzing real-world identity breaches, security teams can identify common attack vectors, understand the impact of poor identity management, and implement stronger defenses to prevent future incidents. These breaches serve as valuable case studies, highlighting the importance of robust identity security strategies.

One of the most well-known identity breaches occurred when a major financial institution suffered an attack that exposed the personal data of millions of customers. The breach was traced back to a misconfigured cloud storage service, which allowed attackers to access sensitive records. This incident demonstrated the risks of improper cloud identity management and the consequences of weak access controls. Many organizations fail to enforce least privilege access principles, granting excessive permissions to cloud resources. Attackers exploit these misconfigurations to move laterally and escalate privileges. Implementing strict identity access management (IAM) policies, continuous cloud security monitoring, and automated remediation tools can prevent similar breaches.

Another significant identity breach involved a social media giant, where attackers successfully exploited weak authentication mechanisms to gain access to high-profile accounts. The attackers used social engineering tactics to manipulate employees into providing access credentials. Once inside the internal systems, they hijacked influential accounts and used them to spread fraudulent messages. This breach underscored the dangers of relying solely on password-based authentication and the need for multi-factor authentication (MFA) enforcement. Organizations must implement strong authentication measures, train employees to recognize social engineering attempts, and use identity threat detection tools to identify suspicious access patterns.

In a different case, a healthcare provider suffered an identity-related breach when attackers exploited stolen credentials from a third-party vendor. The attackers used these compromised credentials to access patient records and billing information. This breach highlighted the risks associated with third-party identity access and supply chain vulnerabilities. Many organizations grant external vendors broad access to internal systems without proper security oversight. Implementing vendor risk management programs, enforcing least privilege access, and continuously monitoring third-party authentication activities are critical to preventing similar breaches. Zero-trust principles should also be applied to ensure that no identity is inherently trusted, regardless of its origin.

Another real-world identity breach involved a government agency where attackers used credential stuffing techniques to access user accounts. The breach occurred because many users reused passwords across multiple services, making it easy for attackers to exploit previously leaked credentials. This incident reinforced the need for password hygiene best practices, such as enforcing strong password policies, using password managers, and implementing adaptive authentication techniques. Organizations should also integrate threat intelligence feeds to detect when employee or customer credentials appear in known data breaches and proactively force password resets when necessary.

A large-scale breach affecting an e-commerce platform revealed the risks of session hijacking and insecure authentication token handling. Attackers intercepted user session tokens and used them to impersonate legitimate customers without needing their passwords. This breach demonstrated the dangers of weak session management and the importance of implementing secure authentication token mechanisms. Organizations must ensure that authentication tokens are properly encrypted, expired after a reasonable period, and tied to a specific device or session. Implementing token binding, endpoint security monitoring, and anomaly detection can help mitigate session hijacking risks.

Another identity breach involving a technology company exposed the risks of insider threats. A disgruntled employee abused their administrative privileges to exfiltrate sensitive data before leaving the company. The breach went undetected for weeks, as there were no effective identity monitoring controls in place. This case highlighted the need for robust insider threat detection strategies, including continuous access reviews, real-time identity analytics, and behavioral monitoring. Implementing just-in-time access controls, where privileges are granted only when needed, can limit the risk of insider abuse. Regular audits and strong logging mechanisms also help detect and investigate suspicious activities.

An attack against a major financial services provider revealed the impact of phishing campaigns targeting executives. Attackers crafted highly convincing emails that impersonated trusted contacts, tricking executives into disclosing login credentials. Once inside the system, the attackers moved laterally, escalating privileges and accessing financial records. This breach emphasized the importance of executive security training, email authentication measures, and phishing-resistant authentication mechanisms. Security teams must deploy advanced email security solutions, enforce FIDO2-based authentication, and use AI-powered detection systems to identify spear-phishing attempts.

A high-profile ransomware attack on a multinational corporation demonstrated the dangers of poor identity segmentation. Attackers initially gained access through a compromised employee account with broad network privileges. They then moved laterally across the organization, deploying ransomware to multiple systems. The breach highlighted the importance of network segmentation, privilege separation, and identity governance. Organizations should enforce strict access controls, limit administrative privileges, and use identity-based microsegmentation to contain potential breaches. Continuous authentication and conditional access policies can also help prevent lateral movement by restricting access based on risk factors.

A retail company's breach exposed the consequences of failing to monitor abandoned or inactive accounts. Attackers exploited an old employee account that had not been deactivated after the employee left the company. Using this account, they accessed payment processing systems and stole credit card data. This breach demonstrated the necessity of regular identity lifecycle management, including timely account deactivation and automated identity cleanup processes. Organizations should implement identity governance frameworks that enforce strict deprovisioning policies, ensuring that unused accounts are disabled promptly.

Lessons from real-world identity breaches emphasize the critical need for proactive identity security strategies. Attackers frequently exploit weak authentication mechanisms, poor access controls, and human vulnerabilities to compromise identities. Organizations must adopt a multi-layered approach to identity security, integrating strong authentication, continuous monitoring, and adaptive identity threat detection. By learning from past breaches, security teams can develop more resilient defenses, reducing the likelihood of future identity compromises.

Identity Risk Assessment Frameworks

Organizations face growing threats targeting digital identities, making identity risk assessment frameworks a crucial component of cybersecurity strategy. These frameworks provide structured methodologies for identifying, analyzing, and mitigating identity-related risks. By assessing identity risks, organizations can prevent unauthorized access, detect anomalies, and strengthen access controls. An effective identity risk assessment framework integrates various factors, including authentication mechanisms, privilege levels, behavioral patterns, and compliance requirements, ensuring a comprehensive approach to identity security.

A fundamental aspect of identity risk assessment is identifying potential threats and vulnerabilities. Digital identities are exposed to numerous risks, such as credential theft, account takeovers, insider threats, and privilege escalation. Organizations must evaluate how identities are created, stored, and authenticated across their systems. This involves analyzing user authentication methods, password policies, and multi-factor authentication (MFA) enforcement. Weak authentication mechanisms significantly increase the risk of identity compromise, making it essential to assess their effectiveness and identify areas for improvement.

A key component of identity risk assessment frameworks is privilege management. Overprivileged accounts pose a serious security risk, as attackers often target them to gain elevated access within an organization. Assessing identity risks requires evaluating whether users have only the permissions necessary for their roles. Organizations should adopt the principle of least privilege (PoLP) to minimize excessive access rights. Privilege creep, where users accumulate unnecessary permissions over time, must be regularly reviewed and corrected. Identity governance solutions help enforce role-based access controls (RBAC) and automate periodic access reviews.

Identity risk assessment frameworks also incorporate behavioral analytics to detect anomalies and potential threats. Traditional identity verification methods rely on static authentication factors, but modern risk assessment models leverage dynamic risk scoring based on user behavior. Machine learning algorithms analyze authentication patterns, device usage, and access locations to identify deviations from normal behavior. For example, if a user typically logs in from a single location but suddenly accesses systems from multiple countries within hours, the framework flags this as a potential risk. Risk-based authentication (RBA) then prompts additional verification or restricts access to mitigate potential threats.

Another critical element of identity risk assessment is continuous monitoring and real-time risk analysis. Cyber threats targeting identities evolve rapidly, requiring organizations to maintain ongoing assessments rather than relying on periodic audits. Security Information and Event Management (SIEM) systems and Extended Detection and Response (XDR) solutions help aggregate identity-related events and provide real-time insights. These platforms analyze authentication logs, failed login attempts, and privilege escalation attempts to detect emerging risks. Continuous risk assessment ensures that identity security controls remain effective in the face of evolving threats.

Risk assessment frameworks must also address third-party and supply chain identity risks. Many organizations integrate with third-party vendors, cloud service providers, and external partners, extending their identity landscape beyond internal employees. Third-party accounts often have access to critical systems, creating additional attack vectors. A comprehensive identity risk assessment framework evaluates the security posture of external identities, enforces strict access controls, and applies conditional access policies. Vendor risk management programs help mitigate the risks associated with third-party identities by requiring compliance with security standards and conducting regular security assessments.

Compliance and regulatory considerations are integral to identity risk assessment frameworks. Organizations must align their identity security practices with regulatory requirements such as GDPR, HIPAA, and PCI-DSS. These regulations mandate strict identity protection measures, including encryption, access control policies, and identity governance. A well-structured identity risk assessment framework ensures that organizations meet compliance obligations while reducing security risks. Compliance audits and identity risk assessments often go hand in hand, helping organizations identify gaps in their security controls and address them proactively.

Identity lifecycle management is another essential factor in risk assessment. Organizations must assess how identities are created, modified, and deactivated throughout their lifecycle. Inactive or orphaned accounts pose security risks, as attackers can exploit them for unauthorized access. An effective identity risk assessment framework includes automated identity provisioning and deprovisioning processes. By integrating identity lifecycle management with identity governance frameworks, organizations reduce the likelihood of security gaps caused by outdated or unnecessary accounts.

Adaptive identity risk assessment frameworks incorporate real-time threat intelligence to enhance security. Cybercriminals frequently use stolen credentials obtained from data breaches, phishing campaigns, or dark web marketplaces. Integrating threat intelligence feeds into identity risk assessment frameworks helps organizations detect compromised credentials and take preventive action. Automated password resets, enhanced authentication requirements, and monitoring of high-risk accounts mitigate the impact of credential-based attacks. Threat intelligence-driven risk assessments provide organizations with a proactive approach to identity security.

Another important aspect of identity risk assessment is risk quantification. Organizations must assign risk scores to different identity-related threats based on their potential impact and likelihood. Identity risk scoring models help security teams prioritize their responses, allocating resources to the most critical risks. For example, an administrator account with access to sensitive data may receive a higher risk score than a standard user account with limited permissions. By quantifying risks, organizations can implement targeted security measures and allocate budgets effectively.

Human factors play a significant role in identity risk assessment frameworks. Employees, contractors, and third-party users often contribute to identity-related security risks through weak password practices, accidental data exposure, or falling victim to phishing attacks. Security awareness training programs must be integrated into identity risk assessment frameworks to reduce human-related risks. By educating users about identity threats and enforcing security best practices, organizations enhance their overall identity security posture.

Incident response planning is another critical component of identity risk assessment. Organizations must prepare for identity-related security incidents by defining response procedures, escalation paths, and remediation actions. When an identity breach occurs, organizations need a structured plan to contain the threat, revoke compromised credentials, and restore affected accounts. Identity threat detection and response (ITDR) solutions complement risk assessment frameworks by providing automated response capabilities. By incorporating incident response planning into identity risk assessments, organizations reduce the impact of identity-related breaches and improve recovery times.

Effective identity risk assessment frameworks continuously evolve to address new threats, regulatory changes, and technological advancements. Organizations must regularly update their frameworks to reflect emerging risks, integrating new security technologies and best practices. By adopting a structured approach to identity risk assessment, organizations enhance their ability to protect digital identities, prevent unauthorized access, and maintain a strong cybersecurity posture.

The Future of Identity Security

Identity security is evolving rapidly as organizations face increasingly sophisticated threats, the rise of decentralized authentication models, and growing regulatory pressures. Traditional security perimeters have disappeared, making identity the central focus of modern cybersecurity strategies. As cybercriminals continue to exploit weaknesses in identity authentication, organizations must adapt by implementing advanced security technologies, adopting zero-trust principles, and rethinking how digital identities are managed. The future of identity security will be shaped by innovations in artificial intelligence, biometrics, decentralized identity models, and continuous authentication techniques.

One of the most significant shifts in identity security is the transition toward passwordless authentication. Passwords have long been a weak point in security, often compromised through phishing, brute-force attacks, or credential stuffing. Organizations are increasingly adopting passwordless authentication methods such as biometrics, hardware security keys, and cryptographic authentication. Technologies like FIDO2 and WebAuthn enable secure authentication without relying on traditional passwords, reducing the risk of credential-based attacks. As passwordless solutions gain widespread adoption, organizations will benefit from both improved security and enhanced user experience.

Decentralized identity is another emerging trend that will reshape identity security. Traditional identity management relies on centralized databases, which are attractive targets for cybercriminals. Decentralized identity models, built on blockchain and distributed ledger technologies, provide users with greater control over their personal data. Self-sovereign identity (SSI) allows individuals to authenticate themselves without relying on third-party identity providers. Instead of storing identity information in a centralized repository, decentralized identity systems enable users to store their credentials securely on their devices. This reduces the risk of large-scale identity breaches and enhances privacy by minimizing data exposure.

Artificial intelligence and machine learning are playing an increasingly important role in identity security. AI-driven identity threat detection systems can analyze vast amounts of authentication data in real time, identifying anomalies and potential security incidents. Behavioral analytics enhance traditional authentication methods by continuously assessing user behavior, detecting unusual login patterns, and triggering adaptive authentication when necessary. AI-powered identity security solutions can also automate incident response, enabling organizations to detect and mitigate identity threats more efficiently. As AI continues to advance, it will become a fundamental component of identity security strategies.

Zero-trust security models are becoming the standard approach for identity protection. The traditional model of trusting users based on network location or static credentials is no longer sufficient. Zero-trust architecture assumes that every access request must be verified, regardless of the user's location or device. Continuous authentication and least-privilege access are core principles of zero trust, ensuring that users only have access to the resources they need at any given time. Organizations are implementing zero-trust frameworks by integrating identity security solutions with endpoint detection, access controls, and risk-based authentication.

The increasing use of multi-factor authentication (MFA) is another key trend in the future of identity security. While MFA has been a security best practice for years, attackers have developed advanced techniques to bypass traditional MFA methods. SIM swapping, push notification fatigue, and adversary-in-the-middle (AiTM) phishing attacks are becoming more common. As a result, organizations are moving toward phishing-resistant authentication methods such as hardware security keys and biometric authentication. Adaptive MFA solutions, which assess risk factors before prompting for additional authentication, will play a crucial role in enhancing identity security.

Cloud identity security is also undergoing significant changes as organizations continue migrating to cloud-based environments. Identity-as-a-Service (IDaaS) solutions provide centralized identity management, allowing organizations to enforce consistent authentication policies across multiple cloud platforms. Federated identity management enables seamless authentication across different cloud applications, reducing the reliance on multiple credentials. However, as cloud adoption grows, attackers are increasingly targeting cloud identity systems. Organizations must implement robust cloud identity security measures, including conditional access policies, identity threat detection, and continuous identity monitoring.

The role of identity governance is expanding as regulatory requirements become more stringent. Data protection laws such as GDPR, CCPA, and emerging global regulations require organizations to implement strict identity security controls. Identity governance and administration (IGA) solutions help organizations enforce compliance by providing automated access reviews, identity lifecycle management, and audit logging. Future identity security frameworks will place greater emphasis on regulatory compliance, ensuring that organizations can manage identities securely while meeting legal requirements.

As digital transformation accelerates, organizations must also address the security challenges of machine identities and non-human entities. The rise of Internet of Things (IoT) devices, robotic process automation (RPA), and API integrations has led to an increase in non-human identities that require authentication and authorization. Machine identity management is becoming a critical aspect of identity security, ensuring that automated processes and connected devices have secure credentials. Organizations must implement identity management solutions that can handle both human and machine identities while maintaining strict access controls.

Privacy-enhancing technologies (PETs) are also gaining traction in identity security. As concerns about data privacy grow, organizations are exploring solutions that minimize the collection and storage of personal data. Techniques such as zero-knowledge proofs (ZKPs) allow users to authenticate themselves without revealing unnecessary personal information. Secure multi-party computation (SMPC) enables collaborative identity verification while preserving privacy. The integration of PETs into identity security frameworks will enable organizations to strengthen authentication while reducing privacy risks.

As the cybersecurity landscape continues to evolve, the future of identity security will be shaped by a combination of technological advancements, regulatory changes, and evolving threat landscapes. Organizations must embrace passwordless authentication, decentralized identity models, AI-driven threat detection, and zero-trust principles to stay ahead of emerging threats. By adopting a proactive approach to identity security, organizations can protect user identities, prevent unauthorized access, and build a more secure digital future.

Cyber Threat Intelligence Sharing for Identity Protection

The rapid evolution of cyber threats targeting digital identities has made threat intelligence sharing an essential strategy for organizations seeking to enhance their identity protection efforts. Cybercriminals continuously refine their tactics, exploiting stolen credentials, leveraging social engineering, and bypassing authentication mechanisms to compromise user accounts. To stay ahead of these evolving threats, organizations must collaborate by sharing cyber threat intelligence (CTI) related to identity attacks. Effective intelligence sharing enables security teams to detect identity-based threats faster, respond proactively, and prevent widespread breaches.

One of the primary benefits of cyber threat intelligence sharing is the ability to detect compromised credentials before they are exploited. Cybercriminals frequently steal login credentials through phishing campaigns, data breaches, and credential stuffing attacks. These stolen credentials are often sold or traded on the dark web, making it difficult for individual organizations to detect when their users' credentials have been exposed. By participating in CTI-sharing networks, organizations can access databases of known compromised credentials and proactively enforce password resets or multi-factor authentication (MFA) for affected users. This preemptive approach significantly reduces the risk of unauthorized access.

Threat intelligence sharing also enhances organizations' ability to identify emerging attack techniques targeting identity security. Cybercriminals are constantly developing new methods to bypass authentication systems, including advanced phishing techniques, man-in-the-middle (MITM) attacks, and session hijacking. By analyzing intelligence from multiple sources, security teams can recognize attack patterns before they become widespread. This shared knowledge allows organizations to implement defensive measures such as phishing-resistant authentication, behavioral anomaly detection, and improved endpoint security policies. Without intelligence sharing, organizations risk falling victim to previously unknown attack vectors.

Collaboration between organizations through industry-specific threat intelligence platforms plays a crucial role in strengthening identity protection. Sectors such as finance, healthcare, and government are prime targets for identity-based attacks due to the sensitive nature of their data. Industry groups and Information Sharing and Analysis Centers (ISACs) provide a structured approach for organizations to exchange identity-related threat intelligence while maintaining confidentiality. These platforms enable real-time sharing of indicators of compromise (IOCs), attack signatures, and tactics used by threat actors. By leveraging collective intelligence, organizations can enhance their defenses and build resilience against identity threats.

Automated threat intelligence sharing has become increasingly important for identity protection. Traditional CTI-sharing methods, such as email reports and manual analysis, are often too slow to counter rapidly evolving identity threats. Security teams now rely on machine-to-machine (M2M) intelligence sharing through protocols such as STIX (Structured Threat Information eXpression) and TAXII (Trusted Automated Exchange of Indicator Information). These standards allow organizations to exchange real-time threat data, enabling automated security responses such as blocking malicious IP addresses, revoking compromised sessions, and enforcing step-up authentication for high-risk users. By integrating CTI-sharing platforms with Security Information and Event Management (SIEM) systems and Extended Detection and Response (XDR) solutions, organizations can rapidly detect and mitigate identity threats.

The integration of cyber threat intelligence with identity and access management (IAM) solutions further enhances identity protection. Modern IAM systems incorporate risk-based authentication mechanisms that adjust authentication requirements based on real-time threat intelligence. If a login attempt originates from a known malicious IP address or is associated with a credential breach, the IAM system can enforce additional verification steps or deny access altogether. This adaptive security approach ensures that authentication processes are continuously informed by the latest threat intelligence, reducing the likelihood of identity compromise.

Threat intelligence sharing also plays a vital role in defending against insider threats. While external attackers pose a significant risk to identity security, insider threats—whether malicious or accidental—can be equally damaging. Employees with privileged access may unintentionally expose credentials through misconfigurations, phishing attacks, or poor password practices. By analyzing threat intelligence related to insider threat patterns, organizations can identify early warning signs of risky behavior. Security teams can then implement proactive measures, such as enhanced monitoring of privileged accounts, just-in-time access provisioning, and behavioral analytics to detect anomalies.

Privacy and data protection considerations are essential when sharing threat intelligence related to identity security. Organizations must ensure that shared intelligence does not expose sensitive user data or violate compliance regulations such as GDPR, HIPAA, or CCPA. Anonymized and aggregated threat intelligence allows organizations to exchange valuable security insights while maintaining user privacy. Many CTI-sharing initiatives employ privacy-preserving techniques, such as zero-knowledge proofs and differential privacy, to enable collaboration without compromising sensitive information. Legal agreements and frameworks, such as the Cybersecurity Information Sharing Act (CISA), provide guidelines for responsible threat intelligence sharing while protecting user identities.

Global collaboration is crucial in the fight against identity-based cyber threats. Threat actors operate across international borders, making it imperative for organizations to participate in global CTI-sharing initiatives. Law enforcement agencies, cybersecurity researchers, and private-sector companies must work together to track cybercriminal activity and disrupt identity-related attack campaigns. International organizations such as Interpol, Europol, and the Cyber Threat Alliance (CTA) facilitate global information sharing, helping organizations combat identity fraud, account takeovers, and credential theft on a broader scale. By fostering international cooperation, security teams can dismantle identity-based cybercrime operations more effectively.

The use of artificial intelligence (AI) and machine learning (ML) in cyber threat intelligence sharing is revolutionizing identity protection. AI-powered threat intelligence platforms analyze vast amounts of authentication data, detecting patterns indicative of identity compromise. These systems continuously learn from new identity threats, improving their ability to predict and prevent attacks. ML models can identify correlations between seemingly unrelated security events, providing deeper insights into complex identity-based attack campaigns. By integrating AI-driven threat intelligence into identity security frameworks, organizations can stay ahead of adversaries and proactively defend against emerging threats.

As identity threats continue to evolve, organizations must embrace cyber threat intelligence sharing as a fundamental component of their security strategy. By collaborating with industry peers, leveraging automated intelligence-sharing platforms, and integrating real-time threat data into authentication systems, organizations can strengthen their identity protection efforts. The collective power of shared intelligence enables security teams to detect identity threats faster, mitigate risks proactively, and build a more resilient cybersecurity posture.

DevSecOps and Identity Threat Mitigation

As organizations accelerate their software development cycles, security must be integrated into every phase of the development process. DevSecOps, a methodology that embeds security into DevOps workflows, plays a crucial role in mitigating identity threats. In modern cloud-native and hybrid environments, identities—whether human or machine—are at the core of security. Attackers frequently target misconfigured identity permissions, exposed credentials, and weak authentication mechanisms to compromise applications and infrastructure. By implementing DevSecOps principles, organizations can proactively identify and mitigate identity-related threats, reducing security risks while maintaining agile development practices.

One of the primary concerns in identity threat mitigation within DevSecOps is securing secrets management. Applications, automation scripts, and cloud workloads often require credentials, API keys, and cryptographic certificates to access services. If these secrets are hardcoded in source code or improperly stored in configuration files, they become prime targets for attackers. DevSecOps teams must implement robust secrets management solutions, such as HashiCorp

Vault, AWS Secrets Manager, or Azure Key Vault, to securely store and manage sensitive credentials. Automating secret rotation and enforcing least-privilege access policies further reduce the risk of identity compromise.

Another key aspect of identity security in DevSecOps is securing the software supply chain. Developers frequently use open-source dependencies, third-party libraries, and containerized applications, which can introduce security vulnerabilities. Attackers exploit weak identity controls in software supply chains to inject malicious code or hijack developer accounts. Implementing software composition analysis (SCA) and dependency scanning within CI/CD pipelines helps detect vulnerabilities in third-party code. Additionally, enforcing code-signing mechanisms and verifying the integrity of software artifacts mitigate risks associated with identity impersonation and software tampering.

Identity and access management (IAM) policies must be integrated into DevSecOps workflows to ensure secure authentication and authorization. Developers, testers, and automated build systems require controlled access to development, staging, and production environments. Without proper IAM enforcement, excessive privileges and misconfigured access controls can expose sensitive systems to unauthorized access. DevSecOps teams should implement role-based access control (RBAC) and attribute-based access control (ABAC) models to restrict user and service permissions based on contextual risk factors. Continuous identity audits and policy-as-code frameworks help maintain consistent security postures across development environments.

The adoption of zero-trust security models within DevSecOps significantly enhances identity threat mitigation. Traditional security models rely on network perimeters, but in cloud-native environments, identity becomes the primary security boundary. Zero-trust principles enforce continuous verification of users, workloads, and devices before granting access to resources. DevSecOps teams should integrate zero-trust identity frameworks, such as Just-in-Time (JIT) access provisioning and continuous authentication, to minimize identity attack surfaces. Enforcing step-up authentication for high-risk activities and implementing machine identity verification further strengthens security.

Another critical factor in mitigating identity threats is securing CI/CD pipelines. Attackers frequently target development pipelines to inject malicious code, steal credentials, or escalate privileges. Protecting pipeline credentials and enforcing strong authentication for developers is essential. DevSecOps teams should implement signed commits, multi-factor authentication (MFA) for source code repositories, and automated security scans in CI/CD pipelines. By continuously monitoring and auditing build processes, organizations can detect unauthorized access attempts and prevent identity-based threats from compromising the software development lifecycle.

Machine identities also present significant challenges in DevSecOps environments. Automated workloads, containers, and microservices require authentication and authorization mechanisms similar to human users. If improperly managed, machine identities can be exploited to gain unauthorized access to cloud resources. DevSecOps teams must implement workload identity federation, automated key rotation, and mutual TLS authentication to secure machine-to-machine communications. Integrating identity governance for non-human identities ensures that service accounts and API keys adhere to least-privilege principles.

Threat modeling is an essential practice within DevSecOps to identify and mitigate identity risks early in the development lifecycle. By conducting identity-focused threat assessments, security teams can evaluate potential attack vectors, such as privilege escalation, credential theft, and insider threats. Implementing security-as-code principles ensures that identity security measures are embedded in application development and infrastructure deployment. Automated policy enforcement tools, such as Open Policy Agent (OPA) and Kubernetes RBAC policies, help enforce identity security at scale.

Monitoring and anomaly detection play a crucial role in mitigating identity threats in DevSecOps environments. Traditional security monitoring tools often fail to detect identity compromises within automated workflows. DevSecOps teams must implement real-time identity analytics using Security Information and Event Management

(SIEM) and Extended Detection and Response (XDR) solutions. By analyzing authentication patterns, failed login attempts, and privilege escalation attempts, security teams can detect and respond to identity threats before they escalate. Integrating security observability within DevSecOps workflows enhances visibility into identity-related anomalies.

Incident response automation is another key component of identity threat mitigation in DevSecOps. When identity threats are detected, security teams must respond quickly to prevent escalation. Implementing Security Orchestration, Automation, and Response (SOAR) solutions allows DevSecOps teams to automate identity-related incident responses, such as revoking compromised credentials, isolating affected workloads, and enforcing adaptive authentication policies. Automated remediation workflows ensure that identity threats are mitigated in real time, reducing the impact of security incidents on development operations.

The shift to cloud-native architectures has introduced new identity security challenges that require continuous risk assessment. DevSecOps teams must adopt proactive security strategies, including identity threat intelligence sharing, continuous compliance monitoring, and cloud access security brokers (CASBs). By integrating identity security into DevSecOps pipelines, organizations can reduce the attack surface, enforce strong authentication controls, and improve overall resilience against identity threats. The combination of automation, continuous monitoring, and zero-trust principles ensures that identity security remains a top priority in modern software development and deployment processes.

Building an Identity-Centric Security Culture

As cyber threats continue to evolve, organizations must adopt an identity-centric security culture to protect their systems, data, and users from identity-based attacks. The shift toward digital transformation, cloud computing, and remote work has made identity the new security perimeter. Traditional security measures that focus solely on network defenses are no longer sufficient, as attackers increasingly target credentials, privileged accounts, and identity verification mechanisms. Establishing a strong identity-centric security culture requires a combination of technological controls, user awareness, governance frameworks, and leadership commitment to ensuring that identity security is prioritized across all levels of the organization.

One of the foundational elements of an identity-centric security culture is fostering awareness and education among employees. Cybercriminals frequently exploit human vulnerabilities through phishing attacks, social engineering, and credential theft. Employees are often the first line of defense against identity-related threats, making it essential to educate them about secure authentication practices, password hygiene, and multi-factor authentication (MFA). Security training programs should go beyond generic cybersecurity awareness and focus specifically on identity threats, such as how to recognize phishing attempts, avoid credential reuse, and detect suspicious login activity. Organizations that invest in regular identity security training reduce the risk of compromised credentials and unauthorized access.

Another critical aspect of building an identity-centric security culture is enforcing strong authentication policies. Password-based authentication remains a weak link in security, as users often choose simple, easy-to-guess passwords or reuse them across multiple accounts. Organizations must implement MFA as a mandatory requirement for all access to sensitive systems. Additionally, the adoption of passwordless authentication methods, such as biometrics, hardware security keys, and adaptive authentication, enhances security while improving user experience. By normalizing these practices, organizations reinforce the importance of identity security in everyday operations.

Leadership commitment plays a crucial role in establishing an identity-focused security culture. Security initiatives often fail when they are perceived as IT-driven projects rather than organization-wide priorities. Executives and senior management must champion identity security by integrating it into corporate policies, risk management strategies, and business objectives. Security awareness should not be limited to technical teams; every department, from human resources to finance, should understand its role in protecting digital identities. When leadership prioritizes identity security, employees are more likely to adopt best practices and view security as a shared responsibility.

Implementing identity governance and administration (IGA) frameworks further strengthens an identity-centric security culture. IGA solutions help organizations enforce least privilege access, ensuring that users only have the permissions necessary for their roles. Access reviews, role-based access control (RBAC), and automated provisioning and deprovisioning reduce the risk of privilege creep, where employees accumulate unnecessary permissions over time. Continuous identity monitoring and access audits provide visibility into suspicious activities, allowing security teams to detect anomalies before they escalate into security incidents. By embedding identity governance into business processes, organizations create a structured approach to managing digital identities securely.

The adoption of zero-trust principles is another fundamental component of an identity-centric security culture. Zero-trust architecture operates under the assumption that no user, device, or application should be trusted by default, regardless of whether they are inside or outside the corporate network. Identity verification is continuously enforced through adaptive authentication, risk-based access controls, and real-time threat detection. Organizations that embrace zero-trust principles encourage employees to take a proactive approach to identity security, understanding that secure access is not based on location or network trust but on continuous verification of user behavior.

Collaboration between IT security teams and other business units is essential for fostering an identity-focused security mindset. Identity security should not be treated as a standalone responsibility of the security team; instead, it should be integrated into human resources, compliance, and operations. For example, HR teams play a key role in identity lifecycle management by ensuring that employee onboarding and offboarding processes include proper identity verification and access deprovisioning. Compliance teams must align identity security policies with regulatory requirements such as GDPR, HIPAA, and SOC 2 to ensure legal and industry standards are met. By involving multiple departments in identity security discussions, organizations create a more cohesive and security-conscious environment.

Security automation is another key factor in building an identity-centric security culture. Many identity-related security breaches occur due to misconfigurations, human error, or delayed incident response. Automating identity security tasks, such as enforcing MFA policies, detecting anomalous login attempts, and revoking access for inactive accounts, reduces the risk of identity compromise. Security orchestration, automation, and response (SOAR) platforms integrate with identity management systems to provide real-time threat detection and response. By incorporating automation into identity security workflows, organizations enhance efficiency while minimizing human errors.

Encouraging a culture of personal accountability for identity security helps reinforce best practices. Employees should feel empowered to report suspicious activity, use security tools effectively, and adopt secure authentication behaviors. Gamification techniques, such as security awareness challenges, phishing simulations, and recognition programs for good security practices, can help increase engagement and motivation. Organizations that create a positive security culture—where employees are encouraged rather than penalized for security-related concerns—see higher adoption rates of identity security measures.

Third-party identity security must also be a priority within an identity-centric security culture. Organizations frequently grant access to external vendors, contractors, and partners, expanding the attack surface for identity threats. Without proper controls, third-party accounts can become weak points in the security ecosystem. Organizations should enforce strict identity verification processes for third-party users, implement just-in-time access provisioning, and continuously monitor third-party authentication activities. Establishing clear policies for third-party identity security ensures that external identities are managed with the same level of scrutiny as internal ones.

As organizations transition toward digital-first business models, an identity-centric security culture becomes a necessity rather than an option. Employees, executives, and IT teams must work together to integrate identity security into daily operations, making secure authentication, access control, and continuous monitoring standard practices. By embedding identity security into corporate culture, organizations enhance their resilience against cyber threats and build a foundation for a more secure digital future.

Implementing an Effective Identity Threat Detection Strategy

The increasing sophistication of cyber threats targeting identities has made identity threat detection a critical component of modern cybersecurity strategies. Attackers continuously refine their techniques to exploit stolen credentials, manipulate authentication mechanisms, and escalate privileges within corporate environments. To defend against these threats, organizations must implement a robust identity threat detection strategy that combines continuous monitoring, behavioral analytics, risk-based authentication, and automated response mechanisms. An effective strategy not only detects identity compromises in real-time but also mitigates potential damage before attackers can escalate their attacks.

A fundamental aspect of identity threat detection is monitoring authentication events across all enterprise systems. Organizations must collect and analyze authentication logs from identity providers, single sign-on (SSO) solutions, virtual private networks (VPNs), and cloud applications. Security Information and Event Management (SIEM) platforms play a crucial role in aggregating authentication logs, detecting anomalous login attempts, and correlating authentication events with other security signals. By continuously analyzing authentication patterns, security teams can identify suspicious activities such as brute-force attacks, credential stuffing, and unauthorized access attempts.

Behavioral analytics enhances identity threat detection by identifying deviations from normal user activity. Traditional authentication methods rely on static credentials, but behavioral analytics adds a dynamic layer of security by analyzing user behavior over time. Machine learning algorithms assess login times, geolocation, device usage, and access patterns to establish a baseline of typical user behavior. When an authentication event deviates from this baseline, the system generates alerts for further investigation. For example, if an employee who typically logs in from a single location suddenly accesses corporate resources from multiple countries within hours, behavioral analytics can flag this as a potential identity compromise.

Risk-based authentication (RBA) is another essential component of an effective identity threat detection strategy. RBA dynamically adjusts authentication requirements based on the risk level associated with a login attempt. If a user attempts to authenticate from an unusual location, an unrecognized device, or after multiple failed login attempts, the system can enforce additional verification steps, such as multi-factor authentication (MFA) or biometric verification. By applying adaptive authentication policies, organizations minimize the risk of unauthorized access while maintaining a seamless user experience for legitimate users.

Multi-factor authentication (MFA) remains a critical defense against identity threats, but attackers have developed advanced techniques to bypass it. Adversary-in-the-middle (AiTM) phishing attacks, SIM swapping, and MFA fatigue attacks have proven effective in circumventing traditional MFA mechanisms. To counter these threats, organizations must implement phishing-resistant authentication methods, such as hardware security keys and FIDO2-based authentication. Continuous identity verification, which extends beyond initial login authentication, further strengthens security by periodically revalidating user identities during active sessions.

Continuous identity monitoring extends beyond authentication events to include privilege escalations, resource access patterns, and account modifications. Attackers often compromise low-privilege accounts and gradually escalate privileges to gain access to sensitive data and critical systems. Privileged Access Management (PAM) solutions provide real-time monitoring of privileged account activities, detecting unauthorized privilege escalations and lateral movement attempts. By integrating PAM with identity threat detection platforms, organizations can enforce just-in-time access controls and automatically revoke excessive privileges when anomalies are detected.

Extended Detection and Response (XDR) solutions enhance identity threat detection by correlating identity-based threats with endpoint, network, and cloud security telemetry. Unlike traditional SIEM platforms that primarily focus on log analysis, XDR provides deeper visibility into identity threats by analyzing authentication events in conjunction with endpoint behaviors and network traffic patterns. If a compromised identity is used to access sensitive files and simultaneously triggers malware execution on an endpoint, XDR can connect these events and trigger an automated response. By integrating identity security with broader threat detection mechanisms, XDR improves detection accuracy and response times.

Insider threats pose a unique challenge in identity threat detection, as malicious insiders already have authorized access to corporate systems. Organizations must implement User and Entity Behavior Analytics (UEBA) to detect unusual access patterns that may indicate insider threats. UEBA solutions analyze historical behavior to establish normal access trends for employees and detect deviations that could signify data exfiltration, unauthorized privilege escalations, or credential misuse. By continuously monitoring identity-related activities, security teams can identify insider threats early and prevent data breaches.

Automating incident response is a critical aspect of an effective identity threat detection strategy. Security Orchestration, Automation, and Response (SOAR) platforms enable organizations to automate identity-related threat responses, reducing the time required to contain security incidents. When a compromised identity is detected, SOAR platforms can automatically revoke access tokens, force password resets, or trigger step-up authentication. Automated response workflows ensure that security teams can react to identity threats in real time, minimizing the potential impact of compromised credentials.

Identity threat intelligence further strengthens detection capabilities by providing insights into known attack techniques, compromised credentials, and emerging threats. Threat intelligence feeds integrate with identity security solutions to detect when employee or customer credentials appear in data breach repositories. Organizations can use this intelligence to proactively force password resets, implement additional authentication requirements, and monitor affected accounts for suspicious activity. By leveraging global threat intelligence, security teams can stay ahead of evolving identity-based attack strategies.

Cloud environments introduce additional complexities to identity threat detection, as organizations must secure identities across multiple cloud providers and Software-as-a-Service (SaaS) applications. Cloud Access Security Brokers (CASBs) provide visibility into cloud authentication activities, detecting unauthorized access attempts and misconfigured identity permissions. Identity threat detection strategies must extend beyond on-premises environments to include cloud-based authentication, ensuring that security teams can monitor and respond to threats in real time across distributed IT ecosystems.

Compliance and regulatory considerations also play a role in identity threat detection. Regulations such as GDPR, HIPAA, and PCI-DSS require organizations to implement identity security controls, monitor authentication activities, and maintain audit logs. Effective identity threat detection strategies align with compliance requirements by providing real-time logging, incident reporting, and forensic analysis capabilities. Organizations that prioritize identity security in their compliance frameworks reduce legal risks while strengthening their overall security posture.

Developing an effective identity threat detection strategy requires a multi-layered approach that integrates continuous monitoring, behavioral analytics, risk-based authentication, and automated response mechanisms. Organizations must adopt modern security technologies, leverage threat intelligence, and enforce adaptive identity security policies to detect and mitigate identity threats before they escalate. By implementing a proactive and intelligence-driven approach to identity security, organizations can reduce the risk of account takeovers, insider threats, and privilege escalations, ensuring that digital identities remain secure in an increasingly complex threat landscape.

Final Thoughts and Next Steps in Identity Defense

Identity security has become the foundation of modern cybersecurity strategies, as organizations face increasingly sophisticated threats targeting user credentials, authentication systems, and access controls. Cybercriminals have shifted their focus from perimeter-based attacks to identity-based compromises, leveraging credential theft, phishing campaigns, and privilege escalation to infiltrate organizations. As a result, organizations must adopt a proactive, multi-layered approach to identity defense, ensuring that digital identities remain secure across cloud, on-premises, and hybrid environments. Moving forward, security teams must prioritize continuous monitoring, adaptive authentication, identity governance, and automation to build a resilient identity security framework.

One of the key priorities in strengthening identity defense is transitioning from reactive security measures to proactive threat prevention. Traditional identity security models have relied heavily on static authentication mechanisms and periodic access reviews, but these approaches are no longer sufficient in an environment where attackers continuously evolve their tactics. Organizations must adopt continuous identity monitoring and risk-based authentication to detect threats in real time. Implementing AI-driven identity analytics helps identify anomalies in authentication patterns, privilege escalations, and unauthorized access attempts before they lead to security incidents.

Zero-trust security frameworks will continue to play a central role in identity defense. The traditional perimeter-based security model, which assumes trust based on network location, has proven ineffective against modern cyber threats. A zero-trust approach enforces strict identity verification, requiring users to authenticate and validate their access continuously, regardless of whether they are inside or outside the corporate network. Implementing zero-trust identity principles involves enforcing least-privilege access, continuously monitoring identity behaviors, and applying just-in-time (JIT) access controls to minimize security risks. Organizations that fully embrace zero-trust security will significantly reduce their exposure to identity-based threats.

As attackers develop new techniques to bypass authentication mechanisms, organizations must enhance their authentication models. Passwordless authentication is gaining traction as a more secure alternative to traditional password-based authentication. Solutions such as biometric authentication, hardware security keys, and FIDO2-based authentication eliminate the risks associated with weak or compromised passwords. Implementing phishing-resistant authentication methods ensures that even if attackers attempt to steal user credentials, they cannot bypass authentication controls. Organizations should prioritize the adoption of passwordless authentication across high-risk applications and privileged accounts.

The integration of identity security with extended detection and response (XDR) solutions provides deeper visibility into identity-based threats. Identity security should not operate in isolation but rather be integrated with endpoint, network, and cloud security telemetry. XDR platforms analyze authentication events alongside other security signals, detecting coordinated attack patterns that may indicate identity compromise. By correlating identity data with broader security events, organizations can improve threat detection accuracy and accelerate incident response. Automated identity response mechanisms, such as revoking access tokens and enforcing step-up authentication, further enhance security resilience.

Cloud identity security remains a top priority as organizations continue migrating to cloud-based environments. Identity-as-a-Service (IDaaS) solutions provide centralized authentication and access management for multi-cloud and hybrid environments, ensuring that security policies are consistently applied across all cloud platforms. Organizations must implement cloud-native identity security controls, including conditional access policies, identity federation, and API security mechanisms, to protect cloud identities from unauthorized access. Continuous auditing of cloud identity permissions helps prevent privilege escalation and misconfigurations that could lead to data breaches.

Identity governance and administration (IGA) will play an increasingly important role in regulatory compliance and security enforcement. Many identity-related breaches occur due to poor identity lifecycle management, where inactive accounts, excessive privileges, or orphaned credentials remain unnoticed. Implementing automated identity governance processes ensures that access rights are continuously reviewed, unnecessary permissions are revoked, and user roles are aligned with business needs. Strong identity governance frameworks help organizations maintain compliance with data protection regulations such as GDPR, HIPAA, and PCI-DSS while reducing the risk of insider threats.

The role of threat intelligence in identity security will continue to expand as organizations seek to stay ahead of emerging threats. Threat intelligence platforms provide real-time insights into compromised credentials, known attack techniques, and adversary tactics. Integrating threat intelligence with identity security tools allows organizations to detect and respond to identity threats before they cause damage. Continuous monitoring of the dark web for leaked credentials enables organizations to enforce proactive security measures, such as forced password resets or adaptive authentication for at-risk accounts.

Another important next step in identity defense is improving employee security awareness and training programs. While technology solutions provide strong identity security controls, human error remains one of the biggest vulnerabilities. Employees often fall victim to phishing attacks, social engineering scams, and credential theft. Organizations must conduct regular security awareness training, teaching employees how to recognize identity threats, use secure authentication practices, and report suspicious activity. Simulated phishing campaigns and real-world security exercises help reinforce good security behaviors and create a culture of identity awareness.

Security automation will be a key enabler of scalable identity defense strategies. As organizations expand their digital footprint, manual identity security processes become unsustainable. Automating identity provisioning, access reviews, and threat response actions reduces human errors and enhances efficiency. Security Orchestration, Automation, and Response (SOAR) platforms help organizations respond to identity threats in real time, ensuring that compromised credentials are quickly revoked and identity-based attacks are contained before they escalate. AI-driven automation further improves security operations by identifying patterns of identity compromise that human analysts might overlook.

Looking ahead, organizations must also consider the impact of emerging technologies on identity security. The adoption of decentralized identity models, powered by blockchain and self-sovereign identity (SSI) frameworks, is expected to reshape the way digital identities are managed. Decentralized identity gives users greater control over their identity attributes, reducing reliance on centralized identity providers that can become single points of failure. While this technology is still evolving, organizations should begin evaluating its potential applications in secure authentication and privacy-enhancing identity management.

As cyber threats targeting identities become more sophisticated, organizations must continuously evolve their identity defense strategies. The combination of zero-trust security, passwordless authentication, AI-driven identity analytics, and security automation will shape the future of identity protection. Security leaders must prioritize identity security investments, integrate identity protection with broader security frameworks, and foster a security-conscious culture among employees. By taking proactive steps to strengthen identity defense, organizations can reduce their risk exposure, protect user identities, and build a more resilient security posture in an increasingly complex digital landscape.